I0634328

Youth Exchanges

THE COMPLETE GUIDE TO THE HOMESTAY EXPERIENCE ABROAD

JOHN HAWKS

Facts On File®

AN INFOBASE HOLDINGS COMPANY

To Dwain McIntosh,

who taught me to love the craft of writing,

and to my mother,

who taught me everything else.

Youth Exchanges: The Complete Guide to the Homestay Experience Abroad

Copyright © 1994 by John Hawks

Facts On File, Inc.
460 Park Avenue South
New York, NY 10016

Library of Congress Cataloging-in-Publication Data

Hawks, John.
    Youth exchanges : the complete guide to the homestay experience abroad /
John Hawks.
        p. cm.
    Includes bibliographical references (p.   ) and index.
    ISBN 0-8160-2922-9 (hc)
    ISBN 0-8160-2923-7 (pb)
    1. Student exchange programs—United States. 2. American students—Foreign countries. 3. Student exchange programs—United States—Directories. I. Title.
LB2376.H38 1994
370.19′62′0973—dc20   93-14178

Text design by Catherine Rincon Hyman
Jacket design by Robert Yaffe
Printed in the United States of America

MP FOF 10 9 8 7 6 5 4 3 2 1

This book is printed on acid-free paper.

Contents

Preface

In December 1982, I mailed a response card from an unsolicited direct-mail brochure about youth exchange programs. Six months later, I took my first airplane ride to Tokyo, Japan—and my first bullet train ride, to Nagoya—for a two-month adventure living as a full-fledged member of the Hara family.

Eleven years later—as the former vice president of a major North American travel trade association, as a writer, and as a volunteer in national youth organizations—I continue to reap the rewards of that unforgettable summer.

Before I left on my exchange, however, I struggled to find reliable information about student exchange programs that would prepare me for what lay ahead. Though several books dealt with college-level programs, my family and I could not locate guides that dealt with youth exchange for high school students. When I returned from Japan, I began outlining what has become *Youth Exchanges*.

My purpose for this book remains the same: Persuading many more young people to make their own exchanges—to discover first-hand that, by living for a time with a family in another country, they can change the world (as the saying goes) one friendship at a time.

Many thanks must go first to the Morita Foundation and the people of McKenzie, Tennessee, for making my exchange possible.

In preparing this guide, I relied heavily on the youth exchange staffers at the U.S. Information Agency, who shared their resources with me and pointed me in the right directions.

I could not have compiled the directory entries without the cooperation of America's youth exchange organizations, who completed survey forms and responded to countless questions. Several groups proved invaluable in arranging interviews with former and current exchange participants.

Susan Schwartz and Michelle Fellner at Facts On File shepherded this book toward publication, investing much time and energy in the process.

Finally, I must thank Anita Diamant, my literary agent, for her leap of faith that resulted in this book.

To those of you who take your own leaps of faith into youth exchange, congratulations on deciding to bring the world closer together.

PART ONE

A Guide to the Homestay Experience

1

Youth Exchange: What Is It?

This year thousands of young people, from Argentina and France to Singapore and the United States, will make a unique, personal, and increasingly powerful dent in world affairs:

- Marti plans to spend her summer in a Japanese "village" of 53,000 people, living with the family of a newspaper publisher. She will attend classes at the local high school, help her sister deliver papers around town on the back of a moped, and even work in a concession stand during the summer festival, making pickled rice balls!

- Randy has captured the memories of a whole year in a stack of photo albums, recording every detail of his life in the Bordeaux wine region of France. To everyone who spares the time to listen, he talks about his experiences working in his host father's vineyard, which has been in the family for seven generations.

- Carey, who will remain in Caracas, Venezuela, for a semester, has tried hard to remember the Spanish he studied at home in Tennessee. As one of the minor characters in the school play at his

Venezuelan high school, he spends his afternoons rehearsing lines for a Latin American version of "Romeo and Juliet."

What do Marti, Randy, and Carey have in common? For a summer, a semester, or a year, they will participate in *international youth exchange programs*: challenging opportunities to learn more about another culture (and mature within their own) by literally living as part of a family, school, and community in another country.

Exchange programs come in all shapes and sizes, from short-term trips lasting for a few weeks to comprehensive year-long curricula. Traditional exchanges place students in individual households, where they do homework, handle chores, and live essentially as another member of the family. Some exchanges have special themes like team sports, with entire groups of players traveling together through another country, competing against native teams and living with different families.

Ask exchange students about their experiences, and they will describe everything from their new classmates to the holiday traditions of their host countries. During their trips, they lived with host families, attended new schools, gained a near-fluent knowledge of other languages, and made many long-lasting friends. Generally their stories will have a common thread: The exchange proved to be one of the most challenging—and most rewarding—times of their lives. Youth exchange translates the basic problems of international relations—misunderstanding, distrust and ignorance—into the daily joys and struggles of family life, allowing these students and their hosts truly to change the world "one friendship at a time."

Exchange programs differ from study tours in two important ways. First, youth exchange emphasizes the *homestay concept*, the chance to experience the daily routine of family life in another country. On the typical tour, tight schedules leave little room for such close contact. Also, the goals of an exchange tend to be *educational*, rather than recreational, in nature. Exchange students can expect to return from the trip with some command of another language, a very personal understanding of the host country's customs, and a renewed sense of their own personal capabilities. In other words, they learn a lot and have fun as well!

THROUGH THE YEARS WITH YOUTH EXCHANGE

The idea of youth exchange did not originate in the United States. In fact, the first "exchange student" began his travels in the Middle East more than 2,500 years ago. The Greek historian Herodotus—known as "the father of history"—journeyed through Syria, Mesopotamia, Babylonia, and Egypt, taking notes about the different cultures he encountered.

Others followed his lead. Aristotle instructed his pupils in the Lyceum to bring back complete descriptions of the various cultures (which he called "constitutions") that they visited during their journeys.

In the Middle Ages, the earliest universities were established, growing steadily stronger as students from many lands flocked to these centers of learning in Bologna, Paris, Oxford, and Salamanca.

During the 17th and 18th centuries, Europe's wealthy noblemen and landowners sent their sons (but not their daughters) on "Grand Tours," capping formal educations with stimulating visits to other countries. Many American colonial families followed suit, especially rich Southern plantation owners. Americans who went on these early exchanges include Charles Carroll, one of the signers of the Declaration of Independence, who journeyed to Belgium, France, and England; William Byrd II, ancestor of polar explorer Richard Byrd, to England; and Benjamin West, noted American artist, to Italy. Throughout the next 150 years, the stream of young Americans going abroad continued.

The homestay concept—facing the challenges of life in another country under the sponsorship of a host family—began in 1932 with The Experiment in International Living (now called World Learning), considered the oldest comprehensive international education organization in the United States. The American Field Service started as a volunteer ambulance service in 1914 to take care of wounded servicemen during World War I; expanding its mission, it began providing intercultural exchanges for secondary school students in 1947.

In 1951, the Department of State asked Dr. Rachel Andresen of the University of Michigan to help make arrangements for 75 young Germans to attend school and live with families in central Michigan for a year. Four years later, 28 Americans went to Germany to spend a year with host families. As government funding for these trips ended, Andresen founded Youth for Understanding, another major exchange group.

Although the number of exchange students remained fairly steady through the years, few Americans really knew much about the whole idea. That began to change on May 24, 1982, when President Ronald Reagan created the Council for International Youth Exchange (CIYE), a consortium of corporations and individuals charged with publicizing exchange opportunities and raising funds to improve existing programs. This push generated a large increase in public interest about youth exchange. During CIYE's first year, a promotional campaign by The Advertising Council gave exchange companies more than $36 million worth of free advertising on the nation's television and radio stations and magazine and newspaper pages. The Consumer Information Center in Pueblo, Colorado, estimates that requests for its free booklet outlining youth exchange opportunities have at times numbered more than 4,000 a month.

With this rise in interest came an explosion in the number of exchange organizations. About half of the groups conducting exchanges in the United States today have been operating for less than 15 years. Many of these new programs are commercial, for-profit travel concerns; others began as nonprofit subsidiaries of larger associations. As more international students enrolled in U.S. schools, and as more American students made plans to go on exchange, both school officials and parents (as well as many established exchange groups) stressed the need to maintain the quality of these programs.

In 1984, the Council on Standards for International Educational Travel (CSIET) was born. This private, nonprofit group develops standards for student exchange organizations, evaluates existing companies, and publishes its Advisory List, an annual "honor roll" of those groups that meet CSIET criteria. "In a nutshell, the Advisory List is the closest thing there is to the 'Good Housekeeping Seal of Approval' in the field of student exchange," said one member of CSIET's evaluation committee. In its 1992–1993 list, CSIET recognized 63 programs that have satisfied the council's basic requirements.

This move toward professionalism has encouraged the continued growth of exchange programs. Citizens exchange arrangements, sister cities projects, and other adult exchanges allow people to participate in this unique cross-cultural activity beyond high school and college. Multilateral exchanges (swaps between countries other than the United States) and the introduction of exchanges to Third World countries underscore the universal appeal of the homestay concept.

THE REASONS FOR YOUTH EXCHANGE

"I am convinced that one of the best ways to develop more accurate perspectives on other nations and on ourselves," said President Reagan, after announcing the CIYE, "is for Americans to join, for a time, a family and a community in another land. In the same way, we cannot hope that other nations will appreciate our country unless more of their future leaders have had the chance to feel the warmth of the American family, the vitality of an American community, and the diversity of our educational system."

Reagan summarized one compelling reason for participating in youth exchanges: *the chance to build mutual understanding and to promote peace.* With advanced technologies (jet airplanes, communications satellites, and fiber-optic telephone lines everywhere) and newly complex perspectives (drug wars that cross continents, mammoth humanitarian events like "Live Aid," the disintegration of the world's Cold War boundaries, and squabbles over trade barriers and protectionism), humanity's problems have become increasingly global, rather than national, in scope. Today, they also seem more hopeless than ever:

> Demographic, economic, political and environmental world trends have combined in recent years to create a qualitatively different class of unavoidable world-level problems that were virtually unknown to traditional diplomacy; that are beyond the reach of national governments; that cannot be fitted into accepted theories of competitive interstate behavior; that are coming increasingly to dominate world affairs; that cannot be wished away; and that are indifferent to military force.
>
> —President's Commission on Hunger, 1980

The hope of finding solutions to these dangers fuels the fire of many exchange groups. "I tell mothers, you are concerned about peace and you think you can't do anything, but you can!" said the late Dr. Andresen. "You can have an exchange student and help that young person to a whole new understanding of our life, our way of thinking, the things that we believe in."

With its heavy reliance on private financial support and volunteer labor, youth exchange can be considered one of the most cost-effective paths to better global relations. As one exchange student wrote, "Probably the greatest part . . . is being able to look at a globe and know I've got friends all over it. Now countries are friends instead of dots on the map."

Beyond the abstract advantages of exchange, students stand to gain practical benefits as well. They will learn how to travel, from securing passports and visas to organizing travel schedules; along the way, they will also develop more self-confidence and tolerance. "Travel is fatal to prejudice, bigotry and narrow-mindedness—all foes to real understanding," Mark Twain wrote. "Likewise, tolerance or broad wholesome charitable views of men and things cannot be acquired by vegetating in one little corner of the earth all one's lifetime."

Exchange programs give students the chance to gain this experience now, before the responsibilities of college, career, and family make a long-term stay impossible. "High school students abroad have a greater opportunity to acquire new perspectives and question personal values than do college students concentrating on academic programs," maintains Ambassador Stephen Rhinesmith in *Assessing Study Abroad Programs for Secondary School Students*.

Youth exchange can lead also to enhanced educational opportunities. More than 50 colleges across the country have scholarships slated specifically for alumni of youth exchange programs. Consider this advice from the director of admissions at a major university: "In a selective admissions process such as ours, this type of overseas experience can be a distinguishing factor, because it says something special about a person's willingness and ability to take advantage of educational opportunities."

Regarding communication abilities, the total immersion in another culture during the exchange can lead a student to a fluent command of the language. In a 1984 survey, educator Gregory Armstrong reported in the *Modern Language Journal* that the mean Advanced Placement (AP) exam score in an exchange student's foreign language was 4.1 (perfect score = 5.0); the College Entrance Examination Board (CEEB) mean score was 710 (perfect score = 800). Seventy-one percent of the students said they began their college language studies at advanced levels, immediately earning 12 to 14 hours of beginning and intermediate credit hours in the language.

Stephen Freeman, an expert in assessing international study programs, has pointed out that exchange students master not only the basics of grammar but also conversational patterns and slang expressions. "A well-run combination of travel and study in a foreign country is an extraordinary incentive and stimulus to further language study after the student returns home. A youngster who has such an opportunity almost invariably wants to continue his study of that country and language after his return," he notes.

Exchange students also learn to get their messages across in more ways than simply by talking. "I came here expecting to learn another language more than anything else," said one returning student, "but now I know that that was not the only goal an exchange student can reach. I don't speak as fluently as I thought I would, but I certainly have learned to communicate."

Coupled with this command of a new language will be a spurt of personal growth that could literally change a student's outlook on life. One major exchange organization outlines these possible results:

Interpersonal Communication—"You may have increased abilities in listening well, speaking clearly, and also paying attention to the expression of non-verbal communication."

Commitment to Persons and Relationships—"You may return with an increased ability to become deeply involved with people, beyond superficial relationships, giving and inspiring trust and confidence, establishing a basis for mutual liking and respect, caring enough for them and acting in ways which are both truthful for them and sensitive toward the feelings of others."

Decision Making—"You may demonstrate increased ability to come to conclusions, based on assessment of the information available, and to take action."

Self-Understanding—"You may return with an increased awareness of and insight into your own learning processes, strengths, weaknesses, successes, failures, biases, values, goals, and emotions."

Self-Reliance—"You may gain a new independence, resiliency, autonomy, willingness to accept responsibility for your own actions, behavior, and education. You may have a receptiveness to new experiences and ideas, a new self-confidence and the ability to function independently."

To support these claims, exchange leaders point to impressive studies such as the one conducted by Dr. Richard Detweiler, president of Hartwick College in Oneonta, New York, who surveyed students participating in a specially funded swap between Japanese and American high schools. Compared with nonparticipants, the exchange students were more likely to select educational and career directions related to international affairs in general and Japan in particular, were more knowledgeable about Japan and Japanese customs, and showed greater achievement orientation and leadership attributes. "The exchange experience has a clear and major impact," Detweiler concluded, "creating a long-term internationalization of the participants. One can certainly assert that international education programs with exchange are invaluable."

Whatever your reasons for considering youth exchange—the chance to help build global relationships, the practical benefits of travel experience and language fluency, or the personal growth that comes from the homestay experience—you should know that making the commitment to the exchange and setting goals for your trip will be just the beginning.

Once you have decided that youth exchange is for you, you can prepare to brave the challenge of your life.

Youth Exchange Students: Why Do They Go?

Some people just can't get enough of a good thing. Jana Riden has proved that point—witness her *three* exchanges!

When she was 14, she perfected her serves and saves as part of a volleyball team that traveled to Holland for competition. During her senior year in high school, she lived overseas with a German family. The following summer, she went to Japan for a two-month exchange.

"I've learned so much through being part of (the exchanges)," Jana said. "I'm definitely more open-minded, more understanding, more mature, much more willing to compromise."

Jana remembered her first trip as a big step in her life. "I'd been to camp before, but that was only for a week, so being away from home for a month was tough sometimes," she said. "But one of my Dutch families really became like a family for me. I look back on the experience and think, 'I really had a great time.'"

After she returned from Holland, her father—a volunteer field manager for a major exchange organization—suggested that she consider going on a year-long homestay. "I thought I'd miss high school, but my year in Germany was such a great experience that high school seemed trivial to me when I returned—and, of course, the year went by too quickly," she said.

Her German exchange gave her a jump on her intended international career. She took 400-level German grammar courses as a freshman at Arizona State University and, based on her exchange experiences, received special permission to study at the University of Tubingen in Germany as a sophomore.

As she completed her degree with majors in German and public relations, she married Michael Schock, a pilot in the German air force completing his training at a Phoenix air base. They moved in February, 1993, to Herne, Germany, where "Jae" (as she is now known) will search for a position as a publications coordinator.

"I really believe [youth exchange] has made me who I am today," she concluded. "It's the smartest thing teenagers can do—the number one choice."

What's it like, running around another country without knowing its language or culture?

"It was pretty scary once I left the group of Americans I had traveled over with. I never had German in school," said Cedric Cunningham of North Carolina, winner of a full scholarship that paid for his summer trip to Germany. "Culture shock set in immediately, due to the language barrier. However, I found that my exchange was the best way to learn another language, because it forced me to use German in everyday situations."

In many ways, he says, he felt welcomed and comfortable as an African American during his stay. For example, when he became confused at a train station about which directions to follow, a 13-year-old girl—who spoke English because it is required learning in German schools—steered him to the correct train.

Cedric returned to Germany in the summer of 1991 for college classes. He intends to join the Peace Corps after graduation, followed by a career as a translator or diplomat.

With a 6–4 record for the season, the average high-school basketball team would not feel very special.

Meet one group of 16 special "globetrotters." Although all of them had played high school basketball in the past, few of them were star athletes. For three weeks, though, they lived together, practiced together and traveled together as one of the first teams of American teenagers to travel to what was then the Soviet Union under a sports exchange program.

Sports-oriented homestays allow students with average or better playing ability to hone their athletic skills, while providing them an enriching exchange experience at the same time.

Playing in Moscow and Tallinn (Estonia), the players compiled a 5–3 record. In Leningrad, the final stop of the tour, they lost their first game but returned to win the final game 75–74 against a very tough team. Coach Randy Hansen keeps that final game sheet framed in his office.

"Our kids were able to meet the Soviet players and go into several homes. They would not have been able to do that without being a part of the basketball team," said Hansen. "We wanted them to understand the culture and become world citizens.

"I have two sons, ages six and nine. As they grow older, I definitely want them to go on exchange. It doesn't matter which country they choose—just that they go."

Would it stretch the point of how beneficial youth exchange can be, if Bianca Moe shares parts of her exchange diary that earned her an *A* in her freshman college English course?

After a year in Venezuela, I now have a place in a wonderful family. And, as an individual, I have become open to new ideas, tolerant of different values and viewpoints, and proud of my own integrity. It will last a lifetime . . .

After a short time in Venezuela, I began to realize that many Venezuelans know a great deal more about the United States than most Americans do about Venezuela. As with other parts of the world, when Latin America makes the news in the United States, it usually involves something negative. However, Venezuela is a peaceful country, with a stable democratic government. Generally, a higher percentage of Venezuelans vote in their national elections than we do in ours. Granted, the region is not problem-free, but the problems Latin America faces are common to many other regions throughout the world . . .

Such conclusions have helped me gain a better understanding and perspective of the world—economically, historically, culturally and politically. Now, for example, I understand that the relationship a Latin American country has with the United States really affects what we hear about that country—and that, in turn, shapes public opinion . . .

The culture is quite different—people have more traditional values, men and women have more clearly defined positions, and the family plays a much more important role in daily life. All this was a bit hard to get used to, but the results were well worth it. Eventually I realized that it was easier for me to accept living in that culture for one year than to attempt to change everyone else's way of thinking, and when that happened I truly became another member of the family. In the process I grew up a lot—and I learned a great deal about myself, my own culture and the United States.

Colleen Chien went to Greece for a summer to learn—and she was not disappointed.

"From the day of my arrival," she wrote during her exchange, "I have gained insights on everything from how to efficiently scrub the floor to the understanding of human nature." Though she remembers standing out in crowds, as one of the few Asian-Americans in her city, "I found it relatively easy to not only observe, but become an active part of the Greek culture—not as a Greek among other Greeks, but as an individual among other individuals," she said.

Living with her Greek family brought a new perspective to Colleen's home life. "I was lucky enough to have two host brothers and a host sister. Within my natural family, I have only one sibling, a younger brother who's seven, but now I have in addition, two older brothers—ages sixteen and nineteen named Eugenis and John respectively, and a younger sister—age eleven named Olivia . . .

"Within the first three days of my stay, I met both sets of grandparents, cousins, aunts and uncles, most of whom I see with a frequency of about three times a week, whereas in the States I see the same relatives about three times a year," she said.

This emphasis on extended families underscored for Colleen a major difference between American and Greek culture. "However, it seems to me that the diversity of American culture is just as essential as is the unity of Greek culture . . . I have just begun to understand this and am learning to look at differences with the question not 'why,' but 'why not?'"

Looking back on her exchange—Colleen is now a sophomore at Stanford University, studying chemical engineering and science policy—she believes it was worth the effort. "Exchange experiences can be very distinct for different students," she said. "What it did for me was provide a total immersion in another culture, without forcing me to lose my own perspective."

———————

Two months in a homestay in the Philippines broadened Judith Carter's outlook on the world—and led to a personal meeting with President Corazon Aquino.

Awarded a full scholarship from the U.S. Information Agency to finance her exchange, Judith left her home in Americus, Georgia, to spend the summer with her host family in Manila. During that time, she saw the poor living conditions which many people faced. "Although many Filipinos may not have the luxuries that we enjoy in the United States," Judith said, "their family ties were much stronger, and respect for their elders was much greater than anything I've ever seen. They are exceptionally caring, helpful and understanding people."

As part of the exchange trip, Judith and four other American exchange students met with President Aquino in her office at Malacañan Palace. During the visit, she welcomed the students to Manila and gave them best wishes for their stay. "Before I went to the Philippines," Judith reflected, "I didn't really care about the rest of the world. My world was Georgia. Now I know I will pay much more attention to developments abroad."

2

Should You Go? A Self-Test Questionnaire

Now that you have learned why Jana, Cedric, Bianca, and other teenagers decided to go on exchange, you should consider joining them. Before you go, however, one major question needs to be answered: "How do I know I'm ready for this?" While there are no surefire tests to determine your potential as an exchange student, the following self-test questionnaire will steer you in the right direction.

INTERNATIONAL AWARENESS

Have you shown interest before in other countries and other cultures?

For example, do you watch TV news programs about world events? Have you made friends with students from different cultural backgrounds who live in your neighborhood or attend your school? Do you like trying different ethnic foods? Have you considered writing letters to an overseas pen pal? Do you enjoy seeing foreign films?

Do you read books and magazine articles about other countries, world history, or famous global figures?

Did you first think about becoming an exchange student after reading a biography of Indira Gandhi or Winston Churchill? Do you catch yourself reading ahead in your world history textbook at school?

Do you speak other languages, or have you decided to take language courses in high school?

As many exchange students discover, being "immersed" in another culture can be the best route to gaining fluent command of a new language. Have you learned a language already from family members or neighbors, or have you proved to be a quick study in your French, German, or Spanish classes in school?

Have you lived in multicultural settings before, in the United States or abroad?

Does your family maintain close ties to an immigrant heritage? Are other languages spoken around your house, besides English? Do you live in a neighborhood, or attend a school, where the residents or students represent different cultures?

PERSONAL MATURITY

Do you consider yourself to be self-confident? How do you handle situations that require strong self-control?

For example, even though you hate speaking in public, can you calm your nerves enough to give oral book reports and other presentations in front of the class? Have you auditioned for plays or the cheerleading squad, despite your fears of not being chosen?

When you have encountered problems in the past, have you shown the ability to adapt to new circumstances?

If your parents have divorced or your family has moved to another city, were you able (after a while) to pick up and move on with your life? Granted, you may not have immediately gotten things under control, but did you finally decide to make the best of your new situation without continually feeling sorry for yourself?

Can you handle being the "minority" in a new culture?

During your exchange, you will probably be one of the few Americans in your host school and city. Will you be able to deal with that feeling of being the center of attention, the "odd man out?"

COMMUNICATION SKILLS

Can you express yourself well—in writing and in speaking?

As an exchange student, you will be forced to pay much more attention to what you say and what you write. It's not necessary that you be a gifted writer or witty conversationalist to succeed; however, you should be able to communicate openly and naturally with your new friends and family.

Are you a good listener?

More important than your ability to express yourself is your ability to listen carefully to what others are communicating to you. Do your friends and family members often confide in you? At school, are you always in the center of the group, talking more than everyone else, or do you consciously pay attention to what others are saying?

Are you skilled at picking up nonverbal cues from other people?

Many times, other cultures rely as much upon nonverbal cues—gestures, facial expressions, and body language—as upon specific words and phrases.

BASIC PREREQUISITES

Are you between the ages of 13 and 18—a high school student?

Generally, the exchange programs described in this directory involve students in grades nine through 12. If you are younger than this age range, chances are you would benefit more from a group program, or a learning vacation taken with your parents, than from a homestay with a host family. On the other end of the spectrum, college students need programs that emphasize—along with the homestay component—courses in certain academic areas (languages, art, sciences) for which they will earn credit at their own universities.

Have you earned good grades in school?

Many exchange groups consider this area very strongly when they interview potential students. Unless you have a C average in your coursework, you should concentrate first on improving yourself at home before you head to a new school overseas.

Now that you have reviewed this questionnaire, you will have a firmer grasp on your chances for success as an exchange student. Like everything else, however, this exercise includes an exception: *The most important qualification is the enthusiastic willingness to give your best efforts to every facet of the exchange.* More than language skills or self-confidence, this commitment will carry you through the exchange and bring the most rewards to you.

3

Youth Exchange: How Do I Choose a Program?

When you have decided to go on exchange, and you have surrounded yourself with stacks of brochures describing the exciting trips awaiting you, be aware of the possibility of getting swindled.

To illustrate the potential hazards of a discreditable program, note the following allegory.

One day, Suzy received a flyer in the mail, describing the summer-abroad programs of a national exchange organization. Caught up in visions of traveling through another country, learning a new language and making friends around the world, Suzy asked her parents about the trip. They agreed to the idea, seeing the exchange as a wise investment of a portion of Suzy's college fund. Immediately, Suzy called the exchange group to request more information; two weeks later, Suzy's family, the Swindleds, returned the signed contract, along with a check for $2,750.

Two weeks before her departure, Suzy received her "orientation materials": a round-trip airline ticket. Mr. Swindled's calls to the organization's national office and regional representative for more information were never returned. Despite her misgivings, Suzy packed her bags and boarded the flight to her host country. Arriving nine hours later, Suzy found no one waiting for her; instead, each teenager wandered around the airport until spotting a family holding the correct nametag. In Suzy's case, there was some initial confusion—her family's placard read "Steve Swindled."

From this discouraging beginning, the visit tumbled swiftly downhill. The teachers in her host school expected her to speak her new language fluently. Her host sisters grew increasingly jealous of the attention that she drew, causing family problems. When things got out of hand, she found that the exchange company had no support staff in the country to give her advice. Within a month of her arrival, Suzy returned home on her own—sadder but much wiser.

Luckily, this unfortunate story does not reflect the experiences of the majority of exchange students, who complete their trips with no major mishaps. Even those teenagers who do have problems are usually able to work out solutions, particularly with the help of qualified counselors and exchange staffers, so that they return with a special understanding of the complex nature of intercultural relationships. However, as with any other large investment of time and money, you should thoroughly investigate exchange programs and the organizations behind them to insure that your visit will be a successful learning experience.

When you begin considering various exchange organizations, dig for concrete answers to these questions:

1. WHO OPERATES THE PROGRAM?

Generally, four types of groups develop, market, and operate youth exchanges:

Commercial—Companies organized to conduct exchanges as independent businesses or as the for-profit arms of tax-exempt groups

Academic—Agencies that function as part of educational institutions, which are usually recognized and evaluated by accrediting associations

Private nonprofit—Independent groups that have received tax-exempt status to carry out exchanges as part of their charitable or educational missions

Special-interest—Organizations that are affiliated with specific religious faiths, fraternal orders, or service clubs, created to operate exchanges that uphold the selective goals and values of the sponsoring groups

What matters most is not the *category* of the group, but rather its *character*.

Researching the group also allows you to plan wisely in applying for admissions and financial aid; for example, an independent commercial operator based in your state could offer special scholarships for residents, while another operation run by your religious faith may tailor programs for members of your church.

No reputable exchange organization will resist answering questions about its background or ownership. Heed the caution flags that fly when you receive evasive, incomplete answers. For every scam operator, however, there are scores of legitimate exchange groups waiting to serve students.

2. WHAT ARE THE GOALS OF THE PROGRAM?

In return for your commitment and hard work as an exchange student, you should expect to reap rewards in these areas:

From **cultural contact**, the awareness and confidence that develop from observing the inner workings—the customs, beliefs, and everyday routines—of another people;

From the **homestay experience**, the formation of close personal relationships and the deep-seated cultural understanding that comes from being treated as a member of a host family;

From **intensive study**, the knowledge gained by learning within the perspectives of another country, especially the fluency in your new language, acquired in your "around-the-clock classroom"; and

From **travel experience**, the ability to handle yourself in adjusting to totally new environments.

When you begin choosing an exchange program, decide first which goals you value most. Then, you can match your interests with the areas highlighted in different programs. Only when you know why you are going on exchange—language fluency, cultural contact, homestay memories, or travel thrills—will you be ready to pick and choose wisely among competing exchange organizations.

3. HOW DOES THE PROGRAM OPERATE?

As an exchange student you should expect that, like other businesses and nonprofit agencies, your organization will run an above-board operation, free of the fits and problems that could spell disaster for your trip. To judge the operating health of your group, insist on straight answers to these questions:

SELECTION

How does the school choose its students?

What are the criteria: year in school, age, grade-point average, special skills like language ability?

Are other characteristics (such as a certain religious faith or state residency) also required?

What steps make up the application process (a comprehensive written application, individual and family interviews, recommendations?)

By what process are host families chosen, and how are the families matched with their students?

What staffers will have responsibility for your visit? What qualifications and levels of experience must they possess to work with the organization?

SCOPE

What are the main components of your exchange—a homestay arrangement, school attendance, special language or skill classes, other forms of cultural contact?

Will you be considered an independent student or (much more likely) a responsible member of a designated host family?

SCHEDULE

When does the program begin? How long does it last: four weeks, a summer, a semester, an academic year?

SUPPORT

Will you undergo an orientation before the trip begins? Is the session planned simply as a crash course in your new culture, or will it also include language training and tips on handling the stresses of being an exchange student?

If you need advice or serious help during your stay, can you count on qualified personnel stationed in your host country?

After you return, will the program offer reentry sessions or other assistance in making the adjustment back?

4. WHAT POLICIES WILL APPLY TO YOUR EXCHANGE?

First, you should check the **financial arrangements** made for your stay. What does the basic program fee cover: airfare, room and board, tuition, language training, and other essential expenses? What additional fees may be charged to you, and what do they cover? Are there expenses not included in the program itself for which you should prepare (*e.g.*, school books and uniforms)? Overall, how does your program fee compare with the prices of similar trips offered by other groups?

Investigate other important financial policies, such as the rules for refunds in the event of cancellation and the provisions for return airfare if you decide to end your exchange early. Many programs insist upon a **code of personal conduct** for their students. What specific situations does that code cover: travel within the host country, the use of drugs and alcohol, smoking? What are the penalties for violating the code?

You do not need the help of a private investigator to find this information. First, *take a very close look at the promotional literature and advertisements of the groups that you are considering*. You can obtain these pieces by writing to the contact person named for each organization whose listing appears in this directory. These materials are designed to attract your interest and to persuade you to go on their exchanges; however, buried in the avalanche of promotion, you will find helpful information like brief program descriptions and lists of fees and financial aid opportunities. You will find this basic information in the directory starting on page 97 of this book.

After you have thoroughly examined this material, *you should continue your search for more objective information from other sources.* Have your language teachers in high school, or the language faculty and international student advisers at area colleges and universities, had any dealings with exchange organizations? If they have, what were their perceptions? Would they recommend any particular group over the others, and why?

Check each company's credentials with two impartial sources:

Have the groups been recognized by the *Council on Standards for International Educational Travel* (CSIET), the industry's watchdog agency? Exchange firms listed with CSIET have been judged by a panel of their peers who base their decisions on the administrative, financial, and educational strengths of each organization and its staffers.

Also, contact the *youth exchange staff at the U.S. Information Agency* to learn about complaints filed against specific groups.

After you have narrowed your choice to two or three organizations, *get firsthand opinions of their programs.* Ask them for *the names of students in your area who have completed exchanges with them.* Also, you should talk with *families who have hosted students from other countries through their programs.* (If the groups point out that their policies do not allow them to reveal these addresses and telephone numbers, request that they have former students and host families contact you directly.) In talking with these people, ask them to describe frankly their experiences and disappointments. You can learn a lot from them.

By this point, you will have ferreted out almost every bit of information crucial to your decision. Now, weigh the choices, make the best call—and then concentrate on your exchange!

4

Youth Exchange: How Do I Prepare for It?

"Making the commitment to the exchange . . . will be just the beginning."

Remember this statement from the end of Chapter One? As you prepare for your trip abroad, wading through medical forms, packing lists, and language tapes, you will begin fighting the second half of the battle.

Now that you have been warned about what lies ahead, however, you can shoulder the tasks of preparing for exchange with a minimum of stress and effort. What is the key? *Take things one challenge at a time.*

PASSPORTS

Your passport will be one of the most important documents you will ever own. Issued by the Department of State, this small navy blue booklet will identify you as a full-fledged American citizen or national, approved for international travel. It is required by law for Americans traveling to other countries (except Canada, Mexico, and several countries in the Caribbean); also, it will serve as a definitive means of identification in banking and commercial transactions. Even when you return, your passport will come in handy for such things as providing proof of citizenship when you begin your first job (fulfilling the "I-9" rules of the Immigration and Naturalization Service).

Recent changes in the application process have sped things up, but since more than 4.3 million Americans request passports each year, you should apply for your passport a full three months before your departure. Because demand for passports increases between January and August, try to submit your application between September and December.

If you have never had a passport issued in your name, you must complete the application (Form DSP-11) *in person* at one of these locations:

> *Major post offices in your state* approved by the State Department to receive applications; OR

> *Any federal court clerk, a clerk of any federal or state court of record, or an official of any probate court*, approved to accept applications; OR

> *Any of the 13 regional U.S. passport agencies.* (Consult the appendix for their addresses and telephone numbers.)

If you are younger than 13 years of age, your parent or guardian must apply in person for you. Teenagers ages 13–17 must be accompanied by a parent or guardian.

First, you will be required to prove your American citizenship. To do that, bring one of these documents:

1. **A passport previously issued to you, or one issued to your parents that includes you** (a type of passport that is no longer valid); OR

2. **A certified copy of your birth certificate**, showing your given name and surname, the date and place of birth, and the fact that the certificate was filed within one year after birth. A delayed certificate (completed more than one year after the date of birth) will be accepted, if it demonstrates that the report of birth was supported by "acceptable secondary evidence of birth."

If you have neither an expired passport nor a certified birth certificate, you will need a **letter from the registrar of the state in which you were born**, proving that your certificate does not exist. Bring this notice along with the best secondary evidence you can show regarding citizenship, such as a **baptismal certificate** or a **hospital birth record**.

Naturalized citizens should present their **naturalization certificate**. Persons born abroad who claim citizenship through a parent must submit either a **certificate of citizenship** from the Immigration and Naturalization Service or a **Consular Certification of Birth** from the State Department.

Along with proof of citizenship, you will need **two** duplicate photographs not more than six months old. They should be nonglossy portrait-type prints, in black and white or color, showing a front view against a plain light background. They must be two inches by two inches in size. (Also, government guidelines suggest, "Photographs which depict the applicant as relaxed and smiling are encouraged.")

Try to have the shots taken by a professional photographer, preferably one who is familiar with the special standards for such shots. Have six to eight prints made; you will need them for your exchange company's records, publicity about your trip, and activities in your host country.

Finally, you should bring with you **some form of personal identification that bears your picture and signature**, like a driver's license or an expired passport. Social security cards, credit cards, and temporary driver's licenses and permits will not be accepted. If you do not have such identification, bring any cards you do have that are issued in your own name; then, your parent or guardian (who must in turn establish his or her own identity with a picture-and-signature ID card) will be asked to sign an affidavit attesting to your identity.

The passport fee for persons under 18 years of age is $40 for a document that is valid for five years from the date of issue. For persons 18 or older, the charge is $65 (which includes a $10 execution fee) for a 10-year passport. (Note: Some post offices and court clerks will not accept cash; you must pay the fee by check, money order, or bank draft.)

If you have had a passport issued in your own name within the last 12 years (and you were at least 18 years old at the time), you may apply by mail to renew it. You must obtain a passport renewal application (DSP-82) from one of the offices listed earlier in the chapter. By certified mail, send your expired passport, the completed application, two photographs, and a check or money order for $55 to the National Passport Center, POB 371971, Pittsburgh, PA 15250-7971. (You do not pay the $10 execution fee in this case.) Keep in mind that you cannot apply by mail if you are requesting your first passport or if your previous passport was issued before your 18th birthday, lost, or stolen.

Again, after you have completed the forms, count on at least two to four weeks to receive your passport, with a longer wait expected during the peak period of late spring through early summer.

Do not carry your passport with you, at home or in your host country, unless you need it to identify yourself. More than 40,000 U.S. passports are lost, accidentally destroyed, or stolen annually. Should that happen to you, file a report immediately with the local police. Then, contact the nearest U.S. consulate or embassy when abroad, or write Passport Services, 1111 19th St., NW, Washington, DC 20522-1705. Also, notify representatives of your exchange organization.

(To make replacement easier, keep a photocopy of your passport pages [showing your name, birthplace, and photograph] in a safe place. With that copy and extra photographs, you can get another passport quickly. The replacement fee is $40 for the five-year version, $65 for the 10-year version.)

In March 1994, the U.S. Passport Service unveiled the next generation of passports: a high-tech version designed to thwart fraud. The visa pages contain imprints of state seals so that each page is unique. Even the inks and paper have special ultraviolet qualities to discourage counterfeiters.

VISAS

While your passport is the primary U.S. travel requirement for Americans going abroad, the visa is the stamp of official permission granted by your host country to enter its borders. Normally, it is just that: an ink mark or other endorsement stamped directly on the pages of your passport. The visa represents approval to visit your host country for a specified purpose (the homestay exchange) and a limited time (as long as one year).

In most cases, you will be responsible for obtaining the proper visas; exchange companies are not legally authorized or equipped to handle that chore. First, remember that you **must have your passport before you can apply for the visa**. Then, check with the nearest embassy of your host country for the specific details of applying for a visa. (The correct addresses and telephone numbers of major embassies in the United States have been listed in the appendix.)

The procedure usually involves mailing your passport to the embassy by certified mail (accompanied in some cases by a visa application and an additional photograph), where officials will stamp the visa in the passport and mail it back. The charge for the visa ranges from nothing to several dollars or more, depending on the country.

Once you have received your passport, plan to apply for your visa six to eight weeks in advance of your trip.

In the appendix is a list of visa services: companies that will take care of your visa application for a charge, ranging from $10 to $45 (in addition to the visa fees). However, unless you plan to visit several countries during your exchange, or your destination is a country that has an intricate application procedure (*e.g.*, nations in the Middle East), these agencies may not be worth your while.

If you will be spending your exchange in a country that requires foreign students to register upon arrival, representatives of your exchange organization or your host parents will help you to take care of this step.

MEDICAL REQUIREMENTS

Getting a full physical examination and updating your immunizations will help you to avoid the risk of health problems that could bring your exchange to an unscheduled end.

First, you must have a very thorough medical examination, including a dental checkup and vision tests. If anything surfaces that might affect the quality of your exchange, discuss the situation with your doctor, parents, and exchange officials.

As an added precaution, join an organization like the Medic Alert Foundation, which records important health information (diabetes, allergies to medications, etc.) for use in an emergency. The initial membership in Medic Alert costs $35; for that fee, you receive a wallet ID card and a necklace or bracelet engraved with your medical condition, identification number, and Medic Alert's address and telephone number. (The annual renewal fee is $15.)

Regarding immunizations, though each country may have varying requirements, you should be completely covered with these shots, which are recommended for all traveling Americans:

Tetanus
Diphtheria
Polio
Typhoid
Measles (both German and rubella)
Mumps
Tuberculosis
Pertussis
Immunoglobin (for viral hepatitis A)

Because most children in America receive these shots before they begin school, all that may be required for you is a series of boosters.

Consult your doctor and exchange officials for additional health information about your host country.

One of the wisest investments you can make in preparing for exchange is the purchase of health insurance coverage for the trip. Already, your family's current policies may protect you fully during the homestay. Check with your parents' employers or insurance agents, however, to determine the limits of that coverage, as well as the claim procedures to follow while you are abroad.

Here are some questions to ask your insurance agent:

What are the limits of my coverage? Determine not only the dollar values given in your policy, but also the types of illnesses and treatments mentioned. For example, some providers cover only short trips abroad, not the extended stays typical of exchanges.

What precise medical expenses are covered? Does your plan provide for hospital care, home health care, prescriptions, and (most important) medical evacuation to you U.S. home, as well as your initial emergency transporation? (Depending upon your location and medical condition, medical evacuation alone can cost as much as $5,000 or more.)

Does the company arrange immediate payments and assistance for you, or does it simply reimburse your family later for expenses that you must pay first?

What sorts of medical documentation and prior approval will be necessary to file claims?

How quickly will help be on hand, and how quickly will claims be processed?

Take with you a copy of the policy and a supply of claim forms.

Plan to carry a full supply of your prescription medicines, especially serums and allergy tablets formulated especially for you or any drugs needed to control a chronic illness. To avoid problems with customs officials, carry these medications in their original containers. Also, have your doctor write a complete prescription, with the generic names of the drugs, and a letter on her stationery explaining your condition and the recommended dosages.

Pack an extra pair of eyeglasses or contact lenses (along with the proper solutions for their care) and a copy of your prescription.

One final word about health: Almost all exchange students complete their programs without any major medical mishaps. Follow these steps so that you can do the same.

ACADEMIC CREDIT

If your exchange is scheduled for a semester or a year, chances are you will be attending school in your host country. For the most part, this opportunity will be one of the most rewarding aspects of your trip; what better way to learn about another culture than studying and making friends with other students in your host country, in their normal, everyday environment?

Unfortunately, these new insights into your host culture will not ease your disappointment when you return home to find that your American school will not accept the coursework you completed during your exchange. *Make sure before you leave home that your school will accept transfer credits from your host school!*

You will be solely responsible for securing this guarantee, under the rules of most programs. Exchange groups will not be able to contact the school boards of every student involved in their trips to check transfer requirements. Once you have decided to make the exchange, contact your school principal or district superintendent to get the exact policies for transferring your work. Your school may need the following information before agreeing to accept your academic work abroad:

1. The *name of the exchange company*, as well as the names of its local representatives, former exchange students in your area, and other schools with which the group has worked

2. The *aims and objectives of the program* (Specifically, your school will want to know the actual *courses* that you will be taking; the

level of instruction, particularly in the sciences and mathematics; the *language of instruction*; and the *duration* of the classes.)

3. The *name and address of the Council on Standards for International Educational Travel* (CSIET) (By writing these groups, school authorities can get answers to their questions about the programs offered by individual organizations, though they do not endorse specific programs.)

Do not wait until the last minute to make these arrangements. Allow plenty of time for your school district to examine your exchange program before deciding whether to grant you credit for your studies abroad.

If you cannot get credit for the classes scheduled during your homestay, then you must decide whether the benefits of your trip outweigh the costs of delaying a semester or year of high school.

PACKING

Unless you have taken many long-distance trips, you will have quite a shock at the actual work of packing for a three-, six-, or 12-month stay in another country. However, taking time to map out your needs will minimize your troubles.

First, select the proper luggage. Most airlines limit the size, weight, and number of bags you can take. Learn about these restrictions before you begin packing. Generally, you should take one medium-sized suitcase and a garment bag, or two medium-sized suitcases, to check as luggage with the airline; they will hold most of your belongings. Also, you can have one or two carry-on bags, ranging in size from an attache case to a combination carry-on/garment bag with compartments for stowing extra clothes, toiletries and important papers. In a carry-on bag, keep the things you will need during your flights: medicine, money, eyeglasses, tickets, candy, a notebook and pen, and your camera with extra film. The only basic requirements are that your bags be lightweight, durable, and easy to carry.

Put ID tags on your luggage. If your group does not provide pre-printed tags, use the blank tie-on tags provided by the airline. Fill in your name and address completely. Also, put an index card with this information inside each bag, in case the outer tag is removed.

In your carry-on bag, keep a complete, itemized list of the contents of every piece of luggage checked with the airline.

In the case of year-long exchanges, you might consider dividing your clothes into warm-weather and cold-weather piles, taking one set with you on the trip and having the other clothes shipped to your host family via air or ship freight. However, investigate shipping fees thoroughly, and insure every package in case of damage or loss.

CLOTHING

Begin your packing in the library, not the mall. Using reference books such as encyclopedias, travel guides, and area studies texts, learn about the average climate in your host country—especially the region in which you will be staying. When you write to your host family before the trip, ask them what types of clothing you should bring; they can give you additional advice about buying school uniforms or clothes for special family trips.

Although jeans and t-shirts will make up most of your everyday wardrobe, you can follow this basic packing list:

M E N

5 casual shirts, t-shirts (some with collars)
5 pairs casual slacks and lightweight jeans
4 pairs shorts
1 formal outfit: blazer, tie, shirt, and slacks
7 changes underwear
2 pairs pajamas
1 pair tennis shoes
1 pair dress shoes
5 pairs socks (dress and athletic)
1 coat
1 windbreaker or athletic jacket
1 warm sweater/cardigan
1 swimsuit

W O M E N

3 casual shirts, T-shirts (some with collars)
3 pairs casual slacks and lightweight jeans
3 pairs shorts
1 coat
1 windbreaker or athletic jacket
1 warm sweater/cardigan

1 bathing suit (not bikini)
1 pair tennis shoes
1 pair dress shoes
3 pairs athletic socks
2 pairs nylons
2 bras
7 changes underwear
Nightclothes
1 dressier dress
3 dresses or blouse/skirt combinations

Leave room in your suitcase for clothes purchased in your host country, such as school uniforms or a new bathing suit.

In addition to clothing, pack these other essential items:

Handkerchiefs/disposable towelettes
Toiletries (including razor blades and deodorant)
Sunglasses
Sanitary napkins/tampons
Makeup and cosmetics

SUPPORT MATERIALS

Before you disappear beneath piles of laundry and clothes hangers, you should also select items that will be fun and useful in explaining your life in America to others.

Here is a list of suggestions that will provide a "little bit of home" while you are gone:

Photo album

Include shots of your family and friends, your house, school and sports activities, and anything else that will help illustrate your American lifestyle to your host family and friends. Concentrate on action shots, not the usual "posed" photographs.

American magazines, history books

Whether the topic is nuclear testing or abortion, the financial markets or new dance steps, many discussions in your new home will center around American culture and current events. A small history text can answer questions about the development of the United States (recommendations:

The Pocket History of the United States, Allan Nevins and Henry S. Commager; *The Pelican History of the United States of America*, Hugh Brotan; and *One Thousand and One Things Everyone Should Know about American History*, John Garraty). News magazines (particularly the international versions of *Time* and *Newsweek*) will give you information to explain current events more clearly. Also, pack a map of the United States, to point out your home state and other places of interest.

Radio, tape recorder

Advances in technology have made available sturdy, compact electronic devices to capture the sounds of your exchange. Use the radio to scan the airwaves in your host country. With the tape recorder, you can catch conversations with your host family, television dialogue, and classroom lectures (to repeat during homework sessions, as you continue learning your new language). You can even dictate "audio letters" to your family and keep an "audio journal" of your exchange.

Sports equipment

A Nerf ball or a Frisbee can provide the perfect excuse for fun with friends at school and your host brothers and sisters.

Favorite books and hobbies

Collecting your host country's stamps and coins, teaching your host mother how to cross-stitch, or re-reading an old classic in a new setting will add another dimension to your exchange.

List of addresses

Through your letters and postcards home, you can share the things you are learning, stay abreast of happenings in America, and keep in touch with friends and family.

GIFTS

Regarding gifts for your host family, it is definitely the *thought*, not the dollar value, that counts. Because your presents will be keepsakes for them, consider carefully what you give them. These gifts should be functional, fairly inexpensive, and representative of life in America, particularly your home region.

Here are some ideas:

Picture books of the United States

Photo books with clear, striking illustrations and descriptive captions are ideal ways to give your host family an overview of the vastness and variety of life in America.

Subscriptions to American magazines

U.S. publications (particularly the international editions of news magazines) can serve not only to keep you informed about current events at home, but also to introduce others to a balanced view of daily news in America.

Food

You may want to prepare a "down home" American-style meal at least once during your stay. Whether it consists of steak and potatoes or hamburgers, French fries, and milkshakes, you should bring with you the recipes of the dishes, as well as special spices and mixes needed. You might choose as one gift a comprehensive U.S. cookbook like those published by Better Homes and Gardens or Good Housekeeping.

Music

While your host family will recognize the names and sounds of the latest pop hits from the radio, they may not own many albums or tapes because they are expensive abroad. You can bring some of the newest releases, along with music from your home region (mountain bluegrass music, for example).

Costume jewelry, "trinkets"

This category includes everything from inexpensive drugstore-variety necklaces and earrings to pen and pencil sets and keychains. Try to find unusual, quality pieces.

Games

Decks of playing cards, travel sets of chess and checkers, and other games will help involve your family in American pastimes and give you something to do on rainy days and long trips.

Unusual gadgets, paper products

Small handmade crafts, new styles of stationery, kaleidoscopes, letter openers, and similar gifts make handy "emergency" presents for forgotten uncles and aunts.

TRAVEL ARRANGEMENTS

Most exchange students will not have the burden of making their own travel arrangements. Airline flight bookings, transfers, and host-country connections will be coordinated by officials of the exchange group. These reservations will be made both for your convenience during the trip and for the maximum savings in travel expenses. Therefore, when you receive your tickets and itinerary, make sure that you understand the schedule and the steps to follow in connecting with your group.

While some students might fly on individual paths directly to their host cities, most organizations transfer their students to gateway airports (such as Seattle for Asian journeys, or New York City for European trips) so that the students may travel as a group. If you have individual flights before you connect with the main group, confirm the arrangements 24–48 hours before the departure time to insure that there have been no changes. As you confirm the flight, check again on baggage limits so that you have no surprises when you arrive at the airport.

Most reputable organizations will meet you at the airport when you make your departure from the United States; in fact, many provide "flight leaders"—adult counselors who have experience working with exchange students—who will make the trip with you to answer questions and to handle travel details. At the other end of the flight, host-country representatives of your organization should meet you at the airport, assist you with clearing customs, and send you on the next leg of traveling to meet your host family.

Try to keep in mind that you will be representing, not only your country, but also your home state, your family, and yourself. Careless attention to travel plans, pranks aboard the airplane, and other rude behavior merely reinforce the world's image of the "ugly American." Remember the primary purpose of your trip: learning more about another culture, another family, and yourself.

Youth Exchange Destinations: How Do I Learn About Them?

Don't be shy in learning about your host country. Make a long list of questions, and work with your exchange representative and other sources to find the correct answers.

Families

What is the size and makeup of the average family?

What is the role of the average teenager?

What is the average daily schedule for fathers, mothers, and children?

Who works in the family?

What are the roles of the father, mother, and children regarding authority, obedience, and decision making?

How do families spend their time together?

What role do elderly people play in families?

What are considered major milestones in life for men and women?

What are the primary differences between families in your host country and in the United States?

Language

What languages are spoken in your host country? What are the major dialects, and where are they spoken?

How many people speak English?

Schooling

Will the schools in your host country be public or private? Coeducational?

Will uniforms be required?

What subjects will be taught?

What extracurricular activities will be available?

How does the average school year run? How long is the average school day?

What are common rules found in most schools?

How are the schools structured? What are the respective roles of teachers and students?

What types of assignments and examinations are common?

What is the average work load for a student?

Money

What is the current exchange rate between the U.S. dollar and your host country's currency?

What coins and bills are used in your host country? What are they called, and what do they look like?

How widely used are traveler's checks and credit cards?

How much do common consumer items costs in your host country as compared to the United States (*e.g.*, food, clothing, cosmetics, cassette tapes)?

Food

How many meals are taken each day, and at what times?

What is the average diet for someone in your host country?

How do the types of foods compare to American favorites?

Are mealtimes important for family relations, or simply for nutrition?

What hygienic concerns exist (purifying drinking water, for example, or peeling fruits and vegetables)?

Clothing

What types of clothing are popular in your host country, especially among students?

What is the appropriate dress for going to school, going out with friends, or going to church?

How does the weather affect your choice of clothing?

What types of clothing are best left in the United States?

Recreation and Leisure Time

What activities will be popular for your host family?

What activities will be popular for students in your host school?

What cultural arts are distinctive in your host country?

Psychology

What things do citizens in your host country strive for—wealth, health, education, cultural attainment?

What type of person is considered an ideal member of your host culture?

What are the respective roles of men and women?

How does your host country view young people? The elderly? The United States?

Community

How is your host country structured, in terms of cities, small towns, and rural areas?

What are the primary industries and businesses for your host country?

How advanced is your host culture in terms of technology: television, telephones, computers?

How are goods marketed in your host country: open-air markets, small stores, supermarkets?

Government

How is your host country's government structured?

What philosophy lies behind the government: democracy, socialism, communism, or a mixture?

What is the system of local government: a mayor, town council, city manager?

Who currently leads the national government?

Gestures

What gestures will matter most for communicating in your host culture?

Which gestures must be avoided altogether?

Holidays and Festivals

What are the dates for special holidays and festivals?

How are these events observed?

What cultural or historical significance lies behind these events?

Religion

What specific religions are predominant in your host culture?

What is the attitude toward religion in general? How tolerant is your host culture toward "minority" beliefs?

Social Customs

What are the rules and boundaries of friendship?

What do high school students do for fun?

From what age does dating begin?

Is dating done in large groups or as couples?

What types of activities are common in dating? Who pays?

5

Youth Exchange: What Will I Do When I Get There?

The most memorable experiences for us were the times when we worked through a particular problem together—discussing a social situation at school, for example, or puzzling over a mispronounced word. Of course, what mattered is not what we did at that moment, but really what we did in terms of deepening our relationship.

How did I know that this exchange worked? Well, when we could sit in the living room comfortably without talking, when we laughed easily at 'strange' cultural behaviors, I realized that things were going well.

Jorge felt at home here, and we felt that he belonged here. That's how we knew things were going well.

—U.S. host mother

When this American host mother describes her year of sponsoring the visit of a Venezuelan student, what she communicates strongly is *joy*: the distinct happiness that wells up when a healthy, stable bond has formed between an exchange student and a host family. This cross-cultural rapport does not happen overnight; it requires careful planning and patient cultivation to make all the factors work. Reaching this kind of close understanding with your host family will be one of your primary challenges as an exchange student.

Most exchange programs are based on the homestay concept, placing students in the homes of volunteering host families or in close contact with them in other settings (taking meals together, for example). Ideally, the student works to become an integral part of the family, engaging in their activities and shouldering typical responsibilities, so that he can learn firsthand the feelings, attitudes, values, and behaviors found in an average family. In turn, the host family gains unique insights into the student's way of life. As the word suggests, this "exchange" of cultural information runs in both directions, dependent upon the commitment of both the family and the student.

The bottom line of exchange success is this: **Each party must surrender something to get something in return.** You will give up independence and cultural security to be included in a warm, caring host family; the family will sacrifice convenience and privacy to grow in its understanding of your culture and to strengthen the ties that bind its own members together.

Do you wonder why a host family would agree to take you in?

- Many families say they want to give students from other countries the chance to experience life in their nation.

- Hosting gives family members a unique opportunity to examine and compare their conceptions and values with someone from another culture, in a trust-filled setting.

- Having a "foreigner" in their midst helps family members to learn more about the world.

- For many parents, hosting satisfies a yearning to make a real contribution to the growth and development of young people— both the exchange students and their own children.

Host families reflect the full range of lifestyles. Some are wealthy, but the majority are middle-class citizens. Some live in large cities, others in medium-sized towns and in small villages, some are childless; others have any number of children of any age. Whatever the situation, your goal is to be treated as a fully participating member of that family. You should not feel pressured to accept your hosts as your "new Mom and Dad," but do not plan on spending the exchange being waited on like a hotel guest. You will be living under new rules and new relationships, governing everything from bathroom schedules to meal times. Take time at the beginning of your exchange to talk with your host parents about the routines and expectations that go with being a part of their family.

Here is a checklist of topics to cover:

Personal and household schedules.   When does the family normally have its meals? Are showers and baths taken in the morning or the evening? Are the weekends reserved for family activities, or will you be free to make plans with friends from school? At what time should you observe the evening curfew?

Personal living arrangements.   Where will you be living and sleeping—in your own space, or with a host sister or brother? Where will you store your clothes and other belongings?

Personal hygiene and dress.   How will you be expected to dress during the week, and when will you need to dress up? Where will you brush your teeth, wash your hair, and keep your dirty clothes?

School and community activities.   Should you check with your family before agreeing to participate in certain school activities, like sports, clubs, and plays? What church and civic groups does the family support, and how can you become involved?

Family standards.   Are there certain areas of conduct in which the family has mapped out preferred ways of behaving? What things might you do that would offend them or hurt their feelings?

After you have uncovered possible conflicts and reached agreement on these issues, you can use the following strategies to develop the close-knit bonds that will make your exchange successful:

Show curiosity about your family's lifestyle.   If you do not understand an event or an opinion, you must ask about it. By agreeing to serve as your sponsors in the exchange, your family expects in-depth discussions of its habits and beliefs.

Share yourself with your family in return.   When significant similarities or differences arise between your conventional way of thinking and your new experiences, talk about them with your host family and friends. Talk as openly as you can about your own family's attitudes and activities.

Help around the house. By washing the supper dishes or weeding the garden, you can show genuine appreciation for your family's willingness to treat you as a full-fledged member of the group.

Try to obey family rules during your stay. Because your host parents have primary responsibility for you during the exchange, you should respect their wishes in such areas as curfew times, household duties, and personal schedules. Discuss with them any rules that make you uncomfortable.

Develop a good rapport with your host brothers and sisters. Think about their position—now they have a new sibling in the house, attracting more attention than anyone else! Like your host parents, your brothers and sisters have made sacrifices in agreeing to open their home to you. Respect their privacy and show interest in their lives as well.

Accentuate the positives in your homestay. Returning exchange students say that the most rewarding moments of their stays came at the strangest times: in the middle of a board game, or in a group dance at the summer festival; during a one-on-one argument with your host grandmother who has never seen an American before; in your new science class, giving your first correct answer in another language. Be on the lookout for these "flashes"; once your exchange has ended, these memories will be the ones most cherished.

Be yourself. The whole point of the exchange for your host family is their exposure to "the average American teenager." Avoid the temptation to act as you think they view American teenagers; instead, be honest yet tactful about your feelings. Remember that the learning curve of the exchange runs in both directions.

Keep saying "thank you." Your host family has made a real investment in your stay, in terms of time, money, and energy. Show your appreciation for this investment, in your words and your actions.

GETTING SETTLED IN

The beginning of your exchange will be a time of great excitement, as well as fear and uncertainty. Everything—food, clothing, living arrangements, your neighborhood—will be brand new, a waiting adventure. Putting the romance aside, though, your first days in your new country will include real physical adjustments. Most exchange students experience very mild discomforts: a sense of fatigue, insomnia, indigestion, and even slight nausea. These ills generally result from the disruption of your regular eating and sleeping patterns. You can expect things to return to normal within a few days.

Along with some physical effects come psychological adjustments. No matter how confident you are when you step off the plane, you will most likely have emotional reactions after settling in, such as disorientation, loneliness, and mild anxiety. While you may continue to feel twinges of loneliness during your stay, these effects tend to wear off quickly. (If they linger, however, refer to the advice in Chapter 6 on dealing with prolonged feelings of homesickness and loneliness.)

To allow time for these changes to run their course, take the first few days easy. Meet your family, and begin talking about their rules and routines. Unpack completely, putting away your clothes and other belongings in your new quarters. Send a note home, to let everyone know that you arrived safely. Explore the house; familiarize yourself with its layout. When you feel especially brave (accompanied by a member of the family, perhaps), scout out your neighborhood; locate nearby stores, the school, the post office, and other points of interest. Greet the neighbors and shopkeepers. Later, you can attempt to use the city's transit system to explore farther.

During these first few days, you might want to begin a journal of your experiences. If you make a firm commitment to keep a complete record of your exchange, you will be able to use this diary later to recall names, faces, and events that became important to you. In addition, keeping a journal is a positive way of working out any feelings or anxieties you may have. In either case, you will be glad for this wise investment of your time.

Show patience in everything during your first few weeks. Keep in mind that you are not the only person making adjustments on this trip; your entire host family has shifted its normal routine to accommodate you. Repay that kindness with a ready smile and plenty of patience.

LANGUAGE

Returning from a year-long exchange trip to Germany, one American senior decided to spend the following summer in Japan on a two-month homestay. To prepare for her visit, she took an intensive course in Japanese, even writing a simple letter to her host family using

Japanese characters. "Too many times, we come across as 'ugly Americans' in our lack of language skills," she noted. "I wanted my family to realize that this exchange is more than a cultural adventure—it will be a language-learning experience as well."

The most advanced videotapes and speaking drills cannot approach the on-the-spot training in another language that you will receive during your exchange. You will be constantly surrounded by your subject. Going hand-in-hand with this rapid learning will be a great deal of frustration, mixed with fear. Faced with the prospect of abandoning English and adopting a brand-new language, you will feel as though your last leg of support has crumbled. Unless you recognize these emotions and deal with them, they can give way to anger, withdrawal, and the failure to adapt completely to your new environment.

Nothing will set a more enthusiastic tone for your exchange than getting off the airplane and greeting your new parents in their native tongue. Learning those introductory phrases, along with other simple words and sentences, before the trip begins will help you to feel more confident upon your arrival. While you cannot be expected to pick up the language instantly, you must plan to spend several weeks of practice before your trip learning the basics.

From that point on, try to make the commitment to use only your new language. Your host family will be eager to work with you as you improve your skills, once they see that you are willing to immerse yourself in their language. Smile a lot, and laugh at your mistakes. Expect good-natured laughter and pats on the back as you make errors; mistakes mean only that you are growing in using your new language.

Because oral proficiency and reading skills are different, they can be acquired best through different approaches. Constant conversations will strengthen your speaking abilities, while a phrase notebook—and even homemade flash cards, made from index cards cut in quarters—will help you to remember the written words.

Find a person in your family or school who speaks English, and use that person as a resource. Ask him to correct your speech when he hears an error and to explain concepts which you do not fully understand. In return, you can do the same for his English-speaking and -writing abilities.

Finally, keep the language barrier in proper perspective. While you will learn an amazing amount of another language in a few months, no one expects you to end your homestay with a full command of it. In fact, you will discover that your host family actually understands your difficulties in adopting their language. Relax—but do not stop practicing at every possible moment!

SCHOOLING

When Rachel James began classes at her host high school in Hamburg, West Germany, she needed every bit of German learned in her two years of language classes. "When I started my homestay, I could only catch a few phrases here and there," she remembered. However, she persisted in her new courses, using German as much as possible, until she broke through the language obstacle in about three months. With her renewed confidence, she began speaking in her classes and joined the school's drama club. "This year in Germany won't necessarily mean I'll get better grades when I get back," she said. "It's simply good for me as a person."

Almost every student participating in a year-long program will have the opportunity to attend classes in the host country. Because the academic year in most parts of the world runs 10 to 11 months, even summer exchange students may attend school. Becoming an "average" student in an overseas high school—mingling with your peers in their classes, at lunch, and during extracurricular activities—will provide you with a very comprehensive opportunity to learn about life in your host country. Immersed in this new atmosphere, you will find that one primary rule of youth exchange still applies: *The harder you try to function as a part of your host culture, the more accepted you will be and the better your experience will be.*

Like your host family, your host school officials will expect you to adopt the responsibilities of native students. You are not in the school as a guest, but as a pupil. Your teachers will have classrooms filled with their regular students; they will not have the time or energy to concentrate on you exclusively. You must do your best to complete the classwork, including homework assignments and special projects. Also, you should get involved in clubs, sports, band and choir, and other extracurricular programs.

Having read that, do not get the impression that you will be thrown into your new school environment, to sink or swim as you can. Your teachers will understand that you are gradually adjusting to a new system and a new language. Beginning slowly, you can continue to improve the quality of your work; if you are having problems in a class, many teachers will arrange special help or even individual tutoring in their subjects. Although your grades may not end up as impressive as they would have been at the end of the year in your home school, you will have gained new knowledge and a new level of confidence that will last long after your grade-point average has been forgotten.

To prepare for this challenge, gather the most reliable information available about schools in your host country. Besides the library, you should consult representatives of your exchange company, your host family, American exchange students who have attended school in your host country, and native students attending school in the United States.

FRIENDS

Years after your exchange, when you thumb through your photo albums, you will discover that certain faces and groups still revive warm feelings of friendship. These relationships developed during your stay can continue long after you have filed those pictures away, adding an international dimension to your life for years to come.

However, many exchange leaders say that friendship is the area in which most students fail to take maximum advantage of their opportunities. To be sure, many stumbling blocks stand in the way of forming these bonds: the new codes of friendship in different cultures; the fact that exchange students sometimes try too hard to "collect" new friends; and the strains of communicating sincerely in an unfamiliar language.

To prepare for this challenge, think closely about the friends you now have and the qualities that you value in them. While the basic concept of "buddies" remains the same the world over, the nature of those ties will vary, according to the people involved and their cultural backgrounds. The roles that they play will depend on their ideas of personal responsibility, exclusivity, their connections with your host family, and even such immutable factors as age, race, and sex.

In making new friends, you can rely upon the guidance of your host family. As in other areas of your homestay, modeling their behaviors and picking up cues from them will help you to catch on quickly to the new rules of the game.

You will have to take the initiative in this game. "You have to realize that foreign people are not going to be climbing all over you to make friends," asserts one returning student. Take that first step by getting involved in the life of your school, studying with other students, and seeking out other teenagers in your neighborhood. The number and depth of your new friendships will depend in large part upon your investment of time and effort.

One caution: Try not to limit yourself to one friend only. While such an arrangement will give you an initial sense of security, it can close you off from chances to meet others. Generally speaking, since the homestay is intended to broaden your outlook, you should form as many satisfying, stimulating friendships as possible—without spreading your time and resources too thinly.

While you are learning these new lessons about life, do not forget your American friends. Keep in touch by sending them quick postcards or a "chain letter" with comments for your whole circle of friends. (Remember to bring along their correct addresses!) Include your new host friends in this circle; show them pictures of your American pals, and describe the things you do with them at home and in school.

Regarding other exchange students, you should agree to plans for an occasional get-together, but avoid the temptation to cling together in a clique. Doing that hampers your adjustment to your host culture and brings feelings of resentment from your family and friends. However, infrequent meetings with other "homestayers" will allow you to relax and compare notes about your experiences.

NEW CUSTOMS AND MORAL CHOICES

As you feel more at home in your new surroundings, you will gain a special sense of accomplishment. You will be learning a great deal about your host nation: its cultural foundations and its history, an appreciation for its views of the world and unique international interests, and its individual customs. Against this background, you must make informed judgments about the various practices and beliefs that you will encounter during the homestay.

Whether your first challenge comes in eating raw fish or drinking wine at dinner, visiting a Scandinavian sauna or attending a Buddhist ceremony, you must prepare yourself for these new situations. Whether your response is intended or not, how you react will have a real impact on your host family and friends. Keep in mind the fundamental rule of cultural differences: These strange habits and beliefs are not better or worse than your own—just different.

By talking with exchange officials, former exchange students, and your host family, you can prepare for the most common cultural differences which you will face. Also, reading one or two books about your host country and its culture is helpful. While you cannot "culture proof" your trip, here are some areas you should monitor:

Hygiene. New experiences like your first Japanese bath—washing and rinsing yourself before entering the tub of scalding hot water, which will be shared in turn by the entire family—will test your resolve quickly! After a few tries at this very relaxing way to bathe, however, you may prefer it to speedy, lukewarm American showers.

Privacy.   Unlike American houses, many homes in other countries do not have enough space to afford solitude to each family member at all times. In fact, it is rare that each person has a separate bedroom, with its own door to shut out distractions. You must find new ways to enjoy peace and quiet (in the yard outside, for example, or at the library) without offending your hosts.

Smoking and drinking.   While a significant number of teenagers in the United States smoke cigarettes, use smokeless tobacco, or consume alcoholic beverages—often with the knowledge of their parents—very few teenagers in other parts of the globe have that freedom. If you use alcohol or tobacco, try to stop before you begin the exchange. If you do, you will find that your stay will be easier.

Food.   "Americans tend to have the idea that every Frenchman eats as though he were having dinner at Maxim's every day," said one French professor. "Living in France, they soon learn that this is not true." From slivers of cuttlefish and kippers in mustard to gazpacho and vichysoisse, your exchange diet will feature new foodstuffs, methods of preparation, and table manners. You will be expected to adapt to these changes, or at least make an honest attempt to do so. You should sample everything offered to you; be considerate yet honest in your responses. Show curiosity about the food; ask how it was selected and prepared. Soon enough, your family will learn your favorite foods and begin understanding your reactions to their normal diet.

Dating relationships.   Most high school students in other countries do not go "steady" with another person; usually, those relationships develop after graduation, at the ages of 17 to 19. During your visit, your friends will concentrate instead on group dates, parties, and school-sponsored events like dances and sports competitions. Indeed, some host parents view dating customs in the United States as rather promiscuous. Therefore, even if you meet Mr. Right on exchange, you might try to confine your romantic contacts to group situations and, later, to letters and phone calls from America.

Religion.   You should decide before your trip begins how you plan to observe your religion in your host country. Unless you are part of a religious order with branches in many parts of the world (such as the Roman Catholic or Lutheran churches), you may have trouble finding a congregation that represents your particular faith. Compounding this choice will be the preferences of your host family. You can achieve balance in this area by attending services with your family and by inviting them to join in your own worship. In any case, prepare yourself for this adjustment by assessing your level of tolerance for other forms of religious expression.

Dress codes.   Choose carefully the styles of clothing which you plan to wear during your exchange. Even though torn t-shirts and jeans, unisex earrings and black athletic shoes are the current rage among American students, your host family may not share your same sense of style.

———

What if you encounter a cultural situation not covered by these guidelines? Follow these steps to work out your answer:

Identify exactly which behavior or value has disturbed you or made you question your own behaviors or values.   Unless you focus on the specific cause for your concern, you could easily exaggerate the problem or overreact to what is actually a minor situation.

When you have isolated the cause, consider what conclusions you have drawn as a result.   For example, if your Brazilian host family appears shocked at your suggestion to cook an American meal for them, have you automatically decided that they must be ungrateful for your offer to share American cuisine with them?

Discuss the situation with the other people involved, describing the behavior or value in question and the ideas that you have developed.   Nothing helps as much as simply talking about your concerns. Avoid the temptation to shrug them off or ignore them; doing so usually aggravates the problem, because you may simply bottle up those feelings until another conflict surfaces. Keeping the lines of communication open with your host family is one of your most critical responsibilities as an exchange student.

Ask them to share their cultural assumptions which led to that behavior or value.   Your Brazilian family may have misunderstood your choice of foods, which included red beans and rice (a New Orleans dish). In their region, some families consider those items peasant foods, and your meal would thus have made them uncomfortable.

Suspend your own views as much as possible, trying to see how the others arrived at their own views.

Compare the two viewpoints, and come to a compromise that works best for everyone. And consider yourself lucky to have gained these insights!

MONEY

Like any major family expense, your trip will require choices and commitments on the part of your parents. Average fees for homestay exchanges range from $1,500 for a summer program to more than $4,000 for a year-long stay, excluding spending money and other incidentals. While many students qualify for scholarships and loans to cover part of the costs, your family will likely spend a significant sum in order to make your homestay possible.

Begin with a reasonable budget. In most cases, your host family will take care of your basic living expenses: food, shelter, transportation during your visit, and other essentials. You will be responsible for spending money, postage, film, snacks, gifts, and other personal items. In addition, some students will have expenses for school uniforms, extracurricular fees, and similar costs.

Your exchange program fee will cover the logistics of getting your exchange set up and concluded. Many program fees also include round-trip international airfares.

Divide your personal budget into three areas: *everyday money*, for snacks, bus fare, and other daily needs; *special trips and purchases*, such as scheduled family outings, overnight stays with friends, and movies; and *souvenirs* for your family and close friends. Then, working with your host family and exchange officials, determine how much money should be allocated for each portion of your budget. Do not worry about bringing large amounts of money, because you will be paying only for out-of-pocket costs (after your program fee has been paid).

Financial problems usually result from two causes: a lack of understanding of exchange rates, or an addiction to needless purchases. First, practice converting various amounts of U.S. dollars into your host country's currency, until you get a good grasp of how far your money will go. Second, resist the temptation to buy everything in sight. Make a list of the persons for whom you will bring back souvenirs. Try not to buy things immediately; instead, take time to shop around, choosing carefully what you will get for each person. A set of postcards, candid photographs of your homestay experiences, or even items like chopsticks or paperback books will often carry more meaning for the people on your list than store-bought tourist trinkets.

Keep an eye on your customs limits, too. Currently, American travelers may bring back $400 worth of merchandise duty-free before they begin to pay penalties. Since your exchange is an educational journey, not a shopping spree, you should have little trouble staying within this limit.

Take money to your host country in the form of generally accepted traveler's checks. An alternative method is having your family send the money via cashier's checks or bank drafts, or through scheduled transfers from your home bank to a new account set up for you in a host bank. Your host family can help you to make these arrangements.

The accepted rule of thumb says that you should convert your dollars to the host currency after you arrive for the exchange. In any case, make transfers only at authorized agencies (banks or government agencies, for example). No black-market deal, no matter how favorable the rate, will be worth the risk of legal penalties and the sudden termination of your trip.

PICTURES AND DIARIES

Do not forget your camera and plenty of film. You can never recapture the pictures of precise moments that, taken together, will give you a cherished record of your time abroad.

Rather than concentrating your shots on the famous places and tourist spots you may visit, use your camera mainly for candid, personal shots. At most attractions and historic sites, you can purchases sets of postcards and slides taken by professional photographers, saving your own film and providing you guaranteed pictures of the places you have visited.

Try to develop your pictures before you return, or ask for hand inspections of your camera bag and film canisters, to avoid problems with airport X-ray machines. Also, keep your photographs or undeveloped film in your carry-on bag; while lost suitcases can be replaced by the airline, lost pictures cannot.

Keep a complete log of your pictures, updating it at least by the end of every roll of film. While you may think you will remember every moment of that special meal or sports match captured on film, you will be surprised how many details fade after a few weeks flooded with other experiences. Note especially the names, dates, and places shown in the pictures.

At the same time, you may want to keep a written journal of your stay. Try to record entries daily, or at least once a week, in a separate notebook. You should jot down buzzwords, names and phrases that describe each day's activities, expanding the entries when you have time. Through this log, you will be able to measure your progress during the exchange, as you have grown in maturity and understanding.

One last hint: Take a supply of manila envelopes with you. As you accumulate large stacks of ticket stubs, interesting ads and magazines, school papers, and other keepsakes, stuff an envelope full and mail it home. This step saves room in your bags—for more pictures and souvenirs!

Youth Exchange:
Stages of the Experience

o grasp the idea of being an exchange student, picture a ride on a roller coaster. Leaving the station, the train of cars in which you are riding gradually climbs to the first large peak; then, it zooms down toward the ground at a dizzying speed before leveling off. The rest of the ride is a series of sharp loops and turns before the cars ease back to the platform at the end.

During your exchange, you will go through a series of challenges—physical, mental, and emotional—as you take your new experiences in stride. Nothing that you read in this guide will make your exchange totally worry-free; however, by understanding the stages through which you will pass, you will be better prepared for the bumps and dips along the way. In their excellent book *Host Family Survival Kit*, Nancy King and Ken Huff have outlined the major phases of a "typical" youth exchange:

1. *Arrival:* The most exciting yet intimidating steps of your exchange will be that walk from the airplane to the terminal in your host country, preparing to turn the corner and meet the people with whom you will be living for the duration of your stay. For the first few weeks, you will continue to feel that sense of exhilaration mixed with doubt—a normal reaction considering the newness of your surrounding environment and culture.

   In this stage, you should concentrate on bolstering your confidence. By studying this guide beforehand, you will be able to anticipate these initial shocks of being transplanted temporarily to another country. For example, hearing your host family greet you in their language will not be unnerving if you are able to respond to their welcome in the same language. No one expects you to speak fluently, but your rehearsed greeting will be a show of consideration that your family will not forget.

Start your exchange by discussing some important topics with your host family:

What names should you call them, and how will they refer to you?

Who occupies which parts of the house? Where are the bathroom, the kitchen, and the living areas? Are there areas of the house which are off-limits?

What is the family's daily schedule? When should you get up in the mornings, and what is your evening curfew? When are meals served?

In what activities will you be expected to help around the house?

Remember two cautions. First, expect some "language fatigue" in the beginning. No matter how much (or how little) of the native tongue you have at your command, there will be times when you want to scream your frustrations—*in English*—at the top of your lungs. However, try to resist the temptation to rely too much on your mother tongue; instead, immerse yourself in your new language. Second, you may experience physical fatigue, particularly in the form of jet lag. Accept this fatigue as a natural part of the traveling process, and get plenty of rest to counteract it. Everything will be new to you at first, from foods and sleeping arrangements to the language and the names which you will call your host parents. This sense of newness can be refreshing and unsettling at the same time.

2. *Settling in:* In this next stage (covering roughly the first two months of a year-long exchange, or the first few weeks of a two-month exchange), you will begin to understand the new rules of the game. When you unconsciously follow the correct route from school to your house without making a wrong turn, and when you raise your hand in class to answer a question, you will feel a new sense of identification and belonging. That feeling shows that your exchange is progressing well. Within this time, however, will come further doubts and misgivings about your stay. Now that you have

passed the first culture shocks, you will notice more subtle contrasts between your own culture and your host surroundings. These discoveries, coupled with any delayed feelings of homesickness that may set in, can lead to anxiety.

When you find yourself faced with this challenge, concentrate on setting realistic goals for yourself during the trip. For example, you may have come to Japan expecting that you would become a standout player on the school's baseball team, based on your prowess in your own school. However, you may find quickly that Japanese teenagers play just as well as your American teammates, leaving you in the dugout during most practices. Your initial reaction could be to spare yourself the agony of staying on the team; but, when you really think about the situation, you may come to believe that what you could learn by staying on the team will be more valuable than any home runs that you might hit for them.

This example illustrates a critical bit of advice about your entire visit. As the exchange progresses, pause from time to time to take stock of your feelings and expectations, then to adjust your behaviors and attitudes to compensate for what you are experiencing.

"Things will be going just right, when they start going a tad wrong!" said one host father in describing this phase. Think ahead so that, when things do go astray, you will be ready to deal with the problem and adjust your goals accordingly.

3. *Deepening the relationship:* If you have ever gone through a disorienting experience, such as moving to a new town, you probably experienced a degree of anxiety. For the first few months, you may have felt uneasy about the new arrangements and avoided making commitments to anyone. After a while, you probably eased into the same schedule, the same activities, that you enjoyed before the changes occurred.

That situation parallels what will happen when you begin deepening the personal ties in your exchange, particularly with your host family. As you arrive and settle in, your primary concerns will be getting through each day as easily as possible. In the next phase, you will begin to plant the roots of friendships and relationships that will keep your exchange going long after you have returned home.

You will have more serious cultural discussions with your family and friends. Before this time, your talks will probably have centered on household schedules and rules; now, you want to understand deeper cultural issues, such as the reasons behind the veils worn by women in the countryside or the festival to celebrate New Year's Day.

In your talks, voice your acceptance of your family and friends, and let them know how grateful you are for this extraordinary opportunity to share their lives with them. Treat these times as learning experiences, more intense and valuable than any classes you might take during the exchange. Understand that this participation in their lifestyle is a two-way street; they will have questions for you. Describe yourself and your customs as completely and unexceptionally as your hosts are doing for you.

When you feel yourself being treated as an accepted member of the family, pulling your own weight in family chores and activities, and when you feel comfortable in the life of your school, then you know that everything in your exchange is on track.

4. *Culture shock:* Of course, there are bumps along every track, especially in youth exchanges. By far, the biggest hurdle for you will be the disillusionment and even the rejection that comes from a good case of culture shock. Culture shock is the condition of anxiety and confusion felt when faced suddenly with an alien culture. More to the point, it occurs when the minor questions raised earlier about customs and beliefs do not lead to deeper relationships, but instead to deeper questions. Your life becomes overloaded with the "newness" of your exchange experience.

What are the symptoms of culture shock?

Being unable to hold a normal conversation with others without feeling rejected or even antagonistic toward the new culture to which you are exposed

Experiencing strong wishes to return home or to stay around other exchange students

Feeling excessive concern about hygiene or personal safety

Having unnatural mood swings

Culture shock is a real condition caused by factors that are largely beyond your control. As this guide prescribes in Chapter Six, the best remedies are discussing your feelings with your family, moving at a more comfortable pace, and understanding that such intense feelings are part of almost every exchange experience.

5. *The holidays:* For students participating in a year-long or fall-semester exchange, the third, fourth, and fifth months bring a special

set of challenges: the holidays. For American students, Thanksgiving and Christmas arrive just as they have begun to conquer the effects of culture shock. Along with the excitement of celebrating these holidays in the style of your host country, this time invites frustration and depression because you will be acutely reminded of home—and how much you miss it.

Here are two hints to ward off holiday blues:

Take part in your host family's holiday traditions. Even though you will naturally spend time reminiscing about your own holiday customs, immerse yourself in preparing for the season with your host family. Besides taking your mind off your absence at home, this attitude will allow you to learn how your host culture observes the holidays. Bringing in the Yule log and leaving straw in your shoes for St. Nicholas' horse will not replace your own customs—but they do afford a new perspective on the universal meaning of these times.

Be prepared for the blues—but try not to give in to them. Prepare yourself for the inevitable: You will feel pangs of homesickness and loneliness during the holidays. However, by realizing that such feelings are normal, you will be sensitive to them. Above all, try not to pass negative emotions to your host family. Talk to them about your feelings, but do not take your frustrations out on them.

6. *Culture learning:* With the proper attitude and a good look at your goals for the exchange, you will weather culture shock and the holidays. From the end of this period until shortly before your departure, you will advance in one of three directions, according to most exchange alumni. Three out of four students either push themselves to new heights of cultural awareness and understanding, or, at the least, complete their homestays without incident. Twenty-five percent of the students in this stage continue to have problems related to culture shock and loneliness, problems that can be traced back to larger concerns about the match between the family and the student or other factors. Usually, these concerns are not extremely serious, but they mean that the students and families must work harder to forge close bonds. Fifty percent of the students continue to strengthen their relationships, learning more and more about their surrounding culture. The final group strikes an upward curve, drawing new vitality from their shocks to gain

even greater results from their exchange experiences.

Wherever you fit on the learning curve, you can take it for granted that this "second half" of your exchange will yield the most concrete results for you. You will have better fluency in your new language; you will feel more enthusiasm; you will begin realizing that the end is approaching for your trip, prompting you to cram more experiences in before you have to leave. Exchange experts King and Huff describe this time as one of "serious introspection, growing pains and heightened cultural self-awareness."

7. *Predeparture:* Sooner than you realize, the final weeks approach before your return home. While there will be a great deal of sadness for everyone involved in your stay, this time will not be altogether negative; in fact, you can tie the loose ends together and put a good ending to a very rewarding period of your life.

You should recognize your feelings for what they are: *sorrow*, at leaving behind these new relationships; *uncertainty*, as you face the return to your native culture crammed full of new information; and *happiness*, at resuming your life at home and seeing your family and friends again. This stage, like the arrival stage, can be a confusing time.

To help put some perspective on your departure, take stock of your exchange in talks with your family and friends, in your journal or in scrapbooks that you have compiled, and in a special dinner or gathering to say goodbye to everyone. You should also be prepared for reverse culture shock.

8. *Readjustment:* You will face a twofold challenge here: making the transition home and sharing the exchange with your family and friends. As with your arrival, however, ease into this stage by talking about your feelings, getting your cultural bearings again, and restoring your memories. Send your host family a note to tell them that you arrived safely. Above all, commit yourself to preserving your new ties; now, you have staked claims in two parts of the world. As one host family told King and Huff:

> "The hosting experience does not come to an end when you say goodbye. You don't just drive home from the airport and resume your normal life. There are feelings to be acknowledged, new routines to be considered and a relationship with your former exchange student which will need defining. All this takes time and work."

6

What Problems Could Come Up?

If you could be linked during the exchange to a computer that recorded your emotions and attitudes every day, the printout for your stay would look something like this graph:

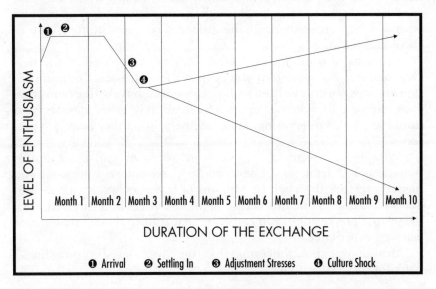

LEVEL OF ENTHUSIASM

| Month 1 | Month 2 | Month 3 | Month 4 | Month 5 | Month 6 | Month 7 | Month 8 | Month 9 | Month 10 |

DURATION OF THE EXCHANGE

❶ Arrival   ❷ Settling In   ❸ Adjustment Stresses   ❹ Culture Shock

1. As you begin the trip, you find yourself filled with enthusiasm about the upcoming exchange (and anxiety, worrying about the surprises waiting for you).

2. That excitement continues and escalates as you settle into your new routine.

3. As time passes, however, the newness of the exchange wears off. You can easily become discouraged or irritated as you experience the stresses of adjusting to your environment.

4. Now comes a critical juncture: You must choose whether you will return to the fast track, enjoying your exchange and learning from your challenges, or you will sink deeper into frustration and depression. For almost every exchange student, this "fork in the road" appears in the form of *culture shock*.

CULTURE SHOCK

Basically, culture shock is the uncomfortable disorientation that stems from the loss of familiar surroundings and means of communication. First, think about your *environment*; you will be living in a place where everything is new to you, from the layout of your house and neighborhood to your daily schedule and family relationships. When the sense of adventure that carried you through the first few days wears off, and when you begin to see beneath the surface of your host culture, culture shock can set in.

In terms of *communication*, even a good command of the new language will not safeguard you against these stresses. Communication involves not only written and spoken words, but also the nonverbal cues, signs, and symbols upon which we rely every day without thinking: modes of greeting, table manners, and other common gestures.

With these beams of support—environment and communication—knocked from under you, you will feel more emotional and mental pressure than before. Millions of travelers and exchange students have undergone this period of intense stress and survived; with the proper preparation, you can even turn culture shock into a major learning experience.

How do you know for certain that you have entered culture shock? Look for these symptoms:

Because you do not know the language (and, perhaps, no one in your family speaks your language well), *you begin to feel like a child when you talk with other people*. At some point, you may resist learning more of the language because the process seems so frustrating.

You show excessive concern about hygiene and safety. For example, you worry about whether unfamiliar foods have been cooked thoroughly, you inspect the cleanliness of your host family's kitchen, or you lock your suitcases before you leave the house.

Minor delays or everyday frustrations make you very tense and irritable, even leading to real anger. You may recognize this stage, for example, if slow busses and trains or long lines in the grocery store bother you more than they normally would.

You begin to depend too much on the company of other Americans, either long-term residents or other exchange students. When you talk with them (in English, of course), you complain about your host country and its "problems."

You experience physical symptoms such as acne, nausea, excessive sleeping, diarrhea, or constipation, which are outward signs of stress, anxiety, or depression.

Generally, your greatest longing is to return to a feeling of "normalness," eating American foods, seeing your own family and friends, and being "at home."

If these signs fit you perfectly, you have a classic case of culture shock. First, *recognize culture shock for what it is—a normal reaction to major changes in your lifestyle.* "Accepting the fact that adjustment is a challenge, but remembering that it is a temporary condition that will pass as you become familiar with the language, mannerisms and local customs, is the first step toward adjustment," say experts with the Language Research Center at Brigham Young University. In many ways, culture shock is a necessary part of the exchange, since going through it teaches you how to adapt successfully to new conditions and how to value the things learned during your trip.

Acknowledging culture shock will be half the battle.

Remember that culture shock stems in part from your newness to the host country, not necessarily from anything your host parents or friends have done to you. Granted, your host family will not be perfect—they will misunderstand you at times and make many mistakes during your stay. But while your hosts should be very supportive, the responsibility to work hard in mastering the new ways of living rests squarely on your shoulders.

Isolate the specific concerns that are causing you trouble. For example, is the entire German language giving you fits, or do you have trouble with a certain set of words that many students do not grasp easily? Have you completely rejected French cuisine, or, as a vegetarian, do you object to eating meat in the dishes that your family prepares? Whatever the case, you will be surprised to find that many major blow-ups can be traced to one small factor.

Once you have discovered the cause, then you can focus your efforts on addressing the problem. Work with a teacher or family member to practice that set of difficult words, or talk with your host parents about your vegetarian beliefs. If the problem proves to be a larger concern than you originally thought, then break the solution down into smaller daily goals, and reward yourself as you hit each one.

Understand that this bout with culture shock will ultimately make your visit much more meaningful. The saying "No pain, no gain" applies here, because culture shock will force you to examine not only the customs of other people but the history and reasons behind them. You will also begin to recognize how your own cultural background has shaped your behaviors and values. Remember—gaining new viewpoints is one reason that you became an exchange student.

Probably the most recurring challenge facing you will be feelings of loneliness and homesickness. For many students, the exchange will be the first major trip they have taken away from their homes and families—and the trip involves much more than just going away to camp for a week or two! Like culture shock, being lonely can be a very normal, expected part of your exchange. The recommended steps for fighting culture shock will work in most cases to control loneliness and homesickness.

Your recovery from culture shock will be evident when you respond easily to cues and symbols in your new environment: the subtle intonations in a conversation, or the unique gestures and expressions that your family uses. Mastering more of the language, you will gain more confidence in dealing with others. Your sense of humor will resurface, and any physical problems will subside. Finally, you will discover a stronger sense of being "at home" in your exchange.

Then, the most important adjustment will happen. "Now that you are willingly adjusting to the new culture," say the Brigham Young officials, "you can accept it as 'just another way' of living. It does not mean that you are enthusiastic about everything the people do or about the way they do it; it does mean that you can accept and understand the differences. You will still have moments of strain and times of misunderstanding, but you will begin to feel more 'comfortable' and will genuinely enjoy yourself."

DEALING WITH LONELINESS

In dealing with and working to overcome loneliness, try to remember that time is on your side. As your homestay progresses, you will form more social connections with your host family and friends. In fact, try to make every attempt to make contact with people, at school, in your neighborhood, and at every other opportunity.

Although your first inclination might be to alienate yourself from others when you're lonely, try to fight this instinct. In order to make friends you'll have to get out and meet people. You may have to make the first move—even though you're the new kid, it's unreasonable to expect everyone to roll out the red carpet for you. You can begin by taking small steps in making friends and by setting reasonable goals for yourself. Instead of trying to befriend the entire soccer team, strike up a conversation with someone you find interesting but know only in passing.

You don't have to worry about your conversational performance. You can make people feel comfortable around you just by appearing relaxed and nonjudgmental. Try to pay close attention to others in conversations. Because you may be dealing with a language barrier try to pick up also on nonverbal cues. Seek out people with common interests similar to your own.

In a limited number of cases, students find that they continue having negative, lonely feelings, to the point that they consider giving up on the exchange. Almost every program profiled in the directory offers a network of trained counselors within the host country; they can provide a sympathetic ear for your troubles and work with you to develop solutions to make your exchange a success.

DEFENDING AMERICA: FIELDING THE HARD QUESTIONS

From fashion to finance, political leaders to television programming, the United States holds a commanding position in many facets of world affairs. Its history, customs, principles, and future are examined and debated around the globe. During your exchange, you could be faced with hard questions that you have never been forced to answer before:

> "Why are so many Americans illiterate?"

> "How do you justify keeping nuclear weapons, when the Berlin Wall has fallen and the Cold War has ended?"

> "What is your country doing to stop drug abuse in your schools and cities?"

For the most part, these questions will come from people who have a genuine interest in learning more about your way of life. At other times, you may face someone with strong anti-American feelings who simply wants to embarrass you when you struggle for a reply. To have the knowledge and confidence to handle these questions, prepare yourself thoroughly by learning more about your own country than you have ever known before.

First, take the list of questions at the end of Chapter 4, designed to help you research your host country, and apply them to the United States. For example, what types of families make up our nation today? How are American schools structured—and how are they changing for the better? In what ways could you describe general U.S. attitudes toward the federal government? Studying these fundamental points of American life will provide you the background to help you answer those tough questions.

In discussions about sensitive issues—AIDS, drugs, illiteracy—remember that no one ever wins an argument. Avoid making prejudicial statements and using exaggerated facts that may turn your talk into a heated battle. In the world of youth exchange, no one's point of view should be considered the best—simply different.

When you talk about issues such as discrimination and poverty, point out the fact that these are *universal* evils; the United States does not have a monopoly on them. Offer your views as one American's way of looking at these concerns, but make it clear that many countries are struggling with similar problems.

Be very reasonable. Find out why questioners are curious about that aspect of your life, and what they already know about it. *Your courtesy and genuine interest in them will be remembered long after your specific answers are forgotten.*

BIG PROBLEMS

In an extremely small number of cases, exchange students encounter situations that could bring their trips to a quick conclusion. Many more mishaps should occur, really, when you consider that exchange organizations move thousands of students each year among different countries; however, the years of experience that they have, and the established support systems that they rely upon, head off most potential troubles. Knowing which bumps may lie ahead will help you not to contribute to those problems—or to cause any new ones yourself.

A. Violations of exchange policies and procedures

Do you remember spending the night with friends and wanting to stay up late, only to have the parents say, "Since we are responsible for you tonight, you must follow our rules and go to bed?" That same reasoning lies behind the policies set by an exchange organization to cover its students. Shuttling many students back and forth, and being charged with insuring that each one receives the proper care and attention, exchange officials must establish ground rules to keep the process running smoothly.

When you investigate different programs, ask the representatives for a complete set of the guidelines which students will be expected to follow. Count it a good sign if they produce a written list of specific rules, since they reflect the experience and stability of that group. Read the list carefully, and ask questions about any policies that are confusing. Here are some of the most standard regulations:

- Except in the limited context of family activities (*e.g.*, wine served with dinner), the use of alcohol will be strictly prohibited.

- Likewise, other than the use of properly prescribed medications or standard remedies like aspirin, students will not be allowed to keep or use drugs of any sort.

- Even if students have valid U.S. driver's licenses and international permits, they should not plan to operate motor vehicles during their stay.

- Unless the scope of the visit goes beyond the limits of the normal homestay exchange (*e.g.*, a college semester abroad), students cannot hold a job in their host country.

- Any run-of-the-mill crimes (such as theft) will not only cause immediate problems like an arrest, but can also lead directly to serious criminal sanctions in the host country. (See the following section on legal troubles.)

- Many programs do not allow students to travel alone in their host country without the express permission of the host family and the exchange company. Likewise, if students travel with their host families, they should notify the exchange representative in their host country before leaving on an extended trip.

- Because excessive contact with your own family can keep you from immersing yourself in your exchange experiences, most groups prohibit a student's "return visit" to the United States, or the parents' visit to the host country, while the exchange is underway.

- Students will probably be terminated from the program if they marry or become involved in a pregnancy during the trip.

- Even with the host family's permission, students will not be allowed to engage in very dangerous activities, such as boxing, bullfighting or skydiving.

- Except under special circumstances (like the death of an immediate family member), students should not plan to return home before, or to remain later than, the scheduled end of their exchange.

While some guidelines may seem very restrictive, keep in mind that the future of your exchange company rests upon the successful completion of hundreds or thousands of individual homestays every year. Only by strictly observing these policies will these groups have any assurance of staying in business, because a string of unfortunate incidents can cause their exchange students and host families, their volunteers and alumni, and the general public to lose confidence in their homestay programs.

B. Legal troubles

The saying "When in Rome, do as the Romans do" takes on special meaning in regard to the legal system of your host country. When you leave the United States to begin your exchange, you become subject primarily to the laws and regulations of your host nation. Although you will remain an American citizen throughout your exchange, that status will bring you limited protection if you are convicted of a crime in your host country. "A passport is a travel document, not a license for a bad trip abroad," said former Secretary of State William Rogers.

To protect yourself, observe this cardinal rule: *Steer clear of any activity that even sounds illegal—including narcotics deals, unofficial currency exchanges, and black-market or clearly "unbelievable" bargains or sales. If you have questions about any situation, consult your host family or exchange officials.*

Particularly devastating would be your suspected use of, or dealing in, illegal drugs or drug paraphernalia. More than 3,000 Americans were arrested abroad last year—and more than 900 of the incidents involved charges of narcotics possession, abuse, or trafficking. In some nations (*e.g.*, Eqypt, Saudi Arabia, Thailand, Malaysia, and Turkey) conviction on these charges leads to a life sentence or the death penalty. Even small amounts of marijuana or cocaine found in the Bahamas brings the punishment of six months in prison, a $2,000 fine, or both. If you are found guilty of a major offense like the possession of drugs, your exchange organization can do little for you except contact your parents (and, then, terminate you from the program). Do not look for much help from officials at the American embassy or consulate; unlike their counterparts in the movies, their hands are also tied. They can alert your family, provide the names of local attorneys who can defend you, and insure that you receive "equitable" treatment under local laws. They cannot arrange bail, provide free legal advice, or get you out of jail.

Do not get involved with drug abuse or other criminal offenses during your exchange.

C. Health problems

Aside from common colds and allergies, there have been cases when students have needed treatment from a doctor or in a hospital during their stay. If you need medical attention, rely upon your host family in seeking help; they can get you quickly to a qualified physician and help in translating your comments if you are not fully fluent in the language. Give the doctor the medical file brought from your own physician; it should show your prior medical history, as well as potential allergies and other essential details.

All medical expenses during your exchange will be borne by you and your own family, not by your host family. To prepare for that eventuality, arrange to pay small expenses directly, then forward the receipts (with a translation) to your parents, along with a completed insurance claim form.

If the bill is beyond your immediate means, send the claim form and receipts to your family immediately so that they can file with the insurance company. In some instances, your parents may be asked to wire or mail a partial payment until the claim is processed. Again, rely upon the guidance of your host family and exchange representatives if the matter becomes that complex.

D. Changing host families

The everyday tensions and disagreements that will crop up during your exchange can develop into serious problems between your host family and yourself. In most cases, students and families reach a deeper understanding of each other's differences; at the least, they can talk through their concerns with the guidance of exchange staffers. However, very major crises can lead to a change in host families. Some exchange organizations admit that as many as one in four of their students will end up being placed with a new family during the exchange.

Authors Nancy King and Ken Huff have described several cases where "re-placements" could work best for everyone involved:

Extremely poor matches between a host family and a student, with irreconcilable differences in lifestyles, interests, and personalities;

Vulnerable "at-risk" students (for example, teenagers with a history of alcohol or drug abuse) who are placed with families not equipped to handle their needs;

Prolonged communication breakdowns (low tolerances for stress and ambiguity, a tendency to ignore problems when they arise, rigid "right-wrong" mentalities);

Antagonism within the family (favoritism or sibling rivalries);

Extenuating circumstances (major illness in the family, loss of employment, or re-location); or

Unmet expectations for the student or the family that cannot be resolved (for example, holding the student to unreasonably high standards of language fluency).

E. Going home

Returning early from your homestay means that one of three things has happened:

You have responded to a grave emergency (an immediate family member has died, or you have become very ill);

You have broken a major policy of the exchange organization; or

You have encountered "irreconcilable differences" several times during your stay, scuttling your chances of a successful exchange.

———————

In the first case, your program will probably cover your expenses in returning home (primarily your airfare). However, if you have contributed greatly to your own troubles during the exchange, you will be terminated by the organization and forced to cover your own travel expenses. By itself, the prospect of springing for a one-way airfare across the ocean should show how important it is to do everything possible to make your exchange work.

The bottom-line advice to follow when things go wrong in your homestay is this: *Identify the root cause, consider your options, and work closely with your host family and your exchange group to find the best solution.* Who knows what you can learn in the process?

I myself have felt badly about my attitudes and participation in (Mexico). Between severe homesickness and problems with my Mexican family I feel I made the worst of what could have been a fantastic learning experience. I did get a lot out of the program, of course. I just feel I could have gotten a lot more. However, I do feel even the 'bad' aspects allowed me to learn *a lot* about myself, and I am very glad I went. Last year in Spain I vowed to make the best of any and all situations I might encounter, and I'm proud to say I came out with flying colors . . . I hope to work abroad eventually. I love working with the Spanish language and can't wait to return to Spain. I'm also eager to travel all over Latin America.

—U.S. exchange student to Mexico and Spain

7

Youth Exchange: What Will Happen When I Get Home?

There's no place like home!"

In *The Wizard of Oz*—arguably one of the first movies about youth exchange—Dorothy Gale returns home to her Kansas farm after surviving the surprises and dangers of her stay in the land of Oz. Despite the challenges of freeing the country from the Wicked Witch's rule and forging several lifelong friendships, she tells her Aunt Em and Uncle Henry that nothing beats the feeling of coming home at the end of a long journey.

Like Dorothy, you will have many new experiences during your stay in another country and feel the same excitement at returning home. Just as Dorothy came back a more mature, understanding person, you will notice differences in yourself as well.

Toward the end of your exchange, spend time reflecting upon the ways in which you have changed. Many "returnee" students say they matured most in these areas:

1. Cultural awareness and understanding

More than learning to use chopsticks or appreciate the bullfights, you have successfully begun to crack the code of another culture. Living like a native-born student, you have gained first-hand knowledge about the way people in another country work and play. You have adapted to a new lifestyle by observing the values and behaviors of your host family and friends, and you know their ways of living are just as valid as your own.

2. Interpersonal communication and relations

Before your trip, you probably never saw the need to improve your speaking and listening skills; in an exchange, though, those abilities became sharper and more focused. You have also learned the importance of nonverbal communications, recognizing cues and gestures that never meant anything to you earlier. Overall, living in a foreign environment forced you to strengthen your communication skills. In today's world—one in which technology and the end of the Cold War have combined to bring about a global market, where neighborhood businesses have accounts around the world—your most valuable asset will be interpersonal skills.

And what about the people with whom you are communicating? You started over again in personal relationships, too, relearning the importance of making commitments, of giving and receiving trust, and of accepting others who have different backgrounds and beliefs. As you finish the exchange, these lessons of sensitivity and tolerance will stay with you, enhancing your family ties and friendships at home.

3. Self-awareness

Being completely transplanted into another country—using a new language, satisfying new responsibilities at home and school, and gaining information about your host culture—made you examine your own self in the process. Every incident has taught you something about your behaviors, your heritage, your thinking patterns, your values, and your goals for the future.

Along the way, you will have abandoned outdated ways of dealing with challenges (like hidden prejudices or mistaken assumptions), and picked up new habits that will serve you better in the world of the 21st century.

4. Self-confidence

Playing center on your host school's basketball team, or performing in your church choir for the first time, requires a certain amount of courage—but that is nothing compared to the bravery needed to go on exchange, uprooting yourself from everything familiar and comfortable. When it hits you that you have lived through the process, you will be amazed at the high levels of self-assurance that you will have. These strong feelings of independence, dependability, and confidence will last long after you return home.

PREPARING TO LEAVE

Like the beginning of your homestay, the departure from your host country will leave you in a state of mixed emotions: *sadness* at leaving your new family and friends, and *excitement* about renewing your ties at home. As you did earlier, keep in mind that these reactions are normal for all exchange students.

As your last hurrah, schedule a farewell meal or get-together with your host family. Since they have made the greatest commitment to your stay, they deserve your undivided attention in sharing goodbyes.

When the final week arrives, confirm your travel arrangements with the help of your host family. Take careful stock of your belongings; consider shipping bulky items and clothing to your home, rather than carrying them on the airplane. In your carry-on bag, store your tickets, medicines, camera and film, and other things you will need during the return trip.

When you reach the airport, you will be drawing to a close one of the most exciting chapters of your life. No matter what happens to you in later years, you will always remember the goodbyes expressed that day, the promises to keep in touch, and the anticipation of returning home.

THE RE-ENTRY PROCESS

Does it sound strange that exchange students might have a difficult time re-adjusting to their normal routines at home? Actually, you may undergo a "reverse culture shock," feeling the same kind of anxiety and uneasiness that you experienced during your homestay. Many things have happened to you since you left home, and in many ways, your family has changed as well. Readjust slowly to the routine; do not try to see everyone and do everything in your first weekend back. Continue keeping your journal during this "returnee" phase. Be understanding when people want to know every detail about your trip. Most important, realize that you will never be the same person you were before you left; no matter where you go or what you do, you will always carry the experience of living in another culture as the legacy of your exchange.

SHARING THE EXCHANGE

As a "returnee," you will shoulder the responsiblity of spreading the good news about your homestay with family, friends, and strangers. From the time that you arrive at the airport—and for weeks on end—you will be peppered with questions about everything that happened to you. Take things slowly at first, but when you feel readjusted, use your photographs and souvenirs to tell the story of your exchange. Not only do you get to share your enthusiasm about your experiences, but you will also remember things about your stay that you had forgotten!

Beyond your family and friends lies another audience: your school. Here are ways to share your exchange there:

- Make short presentations for clubs and classes, using your souvenirs and photographs as visual aids.

- Write an article for your school publication.

- Offer to help work with exchange students in your school. (After all, you know *exactly* how they feel!)

- Do a term paper or research project on your host country and its culture.

CONTINUING THE EXCHANGE

Though the homestay lasted only months, you can extend the excitement of your exchange by staying involved:

1. *Recruit other students.* If you gained so much from your visit, wouldn't other students also reap those benefits? With the help of your guidance counselor or a teacher, meet with students who are interested in going on exchange. Describe your experiences, and

give them an accurate picture of the extraordinary challenges awaiting them. Ask your librarians to make available books from this guide's bibliography that will help them make their decisions.

2. *Provide a home for an incoming exchange student.* With your background as a successful homestay "returnee," you would make a perfect host sibling for a student arriving from another country. Also, you could talk to neighbors, teachers, and other parents about hosting students. (See the following chapter on hosting for more information.)

3. *Serve as an active alumnus of your exchange organization.* Like many educational groups, your exchange company—whether for-profit or nonprofit—depends largely upon the efforts of dedicated volunteers, especially former exchange students in their programs. Based upon your own experience, you can advise students and families about the trials and rewards of youth exchange. Some groups ask their alumni to serve as "big brothers and sisters" to departing exchange students, writing letters and making telephone calls to provide guidance and support. If you live in an area with many "returnees," start an alumni group to share stories and to publicize exchange opportunities in your community. Serve as an adviser to exchange students placed with host families near your home.

   When you volunteer yourself to your exchange group, you will find your hands filled with plenty to do.

4. *Explore exchange opportunities in college and after graduation.* Literally hundreds of college-level programs exist to allow students to travel abroad; many of them feature homestays as part of the overall learning experience. Many programs have been designed to be interdisciplinary, allowing students with various majors to benefit from the trip. While the focus of the trip may not be the homestay experience, you can view it as a chance to see more of the world and its peoples.

   Regardless of whether you take another trip to your host country during school, always maintain your connections there. Take courses in its language, learn to cook its foods, and make friends with its citizens studying at your university.

5. *Explore career opportunities using your exchange skills.* In every direction, today's job market turns with a global spin. From communications and business to science and technology, the fields that will beckon to you upon graduation will require the maturity, decision-making ability, adaptability, and cultural awareness that you acquired as an exchange student.

Even if you never use your new language in your position, the discipline and patience it took to master that language will pay dividends for you in terms of your ability to ride out rough spots in the "real" world.

What will you do when you get home? Reflect on your experiences, rest, and make plans to preserve the value of your exchange for many years to come.

Youth Exchange Alumni: What Happens to Them?

W hat lasting impact will an exchange have, after you have returned home, unpacked, and resumed your normal lifestyle? Beyond the substantial benefits of a broadened world view, more self-confidence, and improved communication skills, other distinct advantages have been discovered by these alumni of exchange programs. They have opened career doors, volunteered their efforts, and shaped new lifelong goals as a result of their time spent in homestay exchanges.

During a recruiting session in 1959, the president of a major exchange organization told John Hansen, "You should do this because it will open the world to you." Hansen spent the following summer living with a family in West Berlin—and he credits that stay with being a "turning point" in his life.

Now, as superintendent of the Dexter, Michigan, public schools, Hansen appreciates the personal growth he sees in returning exchange students. "The homestay provides a forced awakening for them," he says. "Our young people need to learn to compete in a global economy, but it's really not a small world to you if you haven't been anywhere."

Seeing new challenges in the future for youth exchange—including the task of increasing the number of homestays in developing countries—Hansen trains volunteer area representatives for the company that sent him to Germany more than 30 years ago. "If I don't refill the well, it will run dry," he says.

Paul Robson of Seattle credits his knowledge of Germany and its language—acquired during an exchange in 1978—with helping him to launch a career with Microsoft Corporation, the world's largest manufacturer of computer software.

Beginning as a technical writer translating Microsoft product manuals into German versions, Robson moved to Munich in 1989 to lead the introduction of new software programs in Russian. One year later, he was promoted to marketing manager in charge of sales for Eastern Europe.

"Corporate America would do well to look even more closely at the benefits of youth exchange and dedicate more resources to its support," he says. "Young people who have spent time abroad are the ideal workforce of the future. Not only do they invariably go on to become influential leaders; they also acquire the communication skills, flexibility, and cultural awareness which are vital for success in the business world of the next century."

In March 1993, Robson decided to leave Microsoft to pursue another dream: writing fiction in English and, later, German from his Munich home. "The path which I chose as a 17-year-old in 1978 has resulted in an exciting international career, close friendships with people throughout the world, and an outlook on life which is ideally suited to the rapidly changing world of the 1990s and beyond."

Sherry Paul still remembers her first day in France. "When I stepped out of the Paris metro," she says, "and I saw the Arc de Triomphe, it was a magical moment. I had been reading about it and looking at pictures all through school, and now its glory and magnificence were standing before me."

Twenty years later, as a senior vice president for one of the world's largest advertising agencies, her adaptive nature and strong communication skills have given her a stellar career. *Advertising Age* magazine named her one of its "100 Best and Brightest Women in Advertising."

"Being an exchange student was a very broadening experience," says Mrs. Paul. "I grew up in the conservative Midwest, so it was through my exchange that I learned that the U.S. is just one small part of the world.

"I deal all the time with people who think differently from me. I have a business mindset and people like copywriters and art directors have different approaches to issues, just as people from other countries have different views. I've learned how to communicate with them effectively and be more persuasive.

"I know my exchange helped me more than I realized at the time."

8

Youth Exchange: What About Parents?

In this book you have covered the essential topics for a successful exchange experience: the values and benefits you will reap, the preparations you must make for the trip, the stages you will pass through, and the challenges you will face when you return. What has not been discussed is one of the most critical factors in the whole process: *your parents*. They will help you make decisions about your exchange and pay for the trip; then, they will lose you for several months (perhaps your longest trip away from home), only to have you return a different person, more worldly and mature than before. In many ways, they will be as involved in the exchange as you are.

Therefore, this chapter will be directed toward them, so that they understand their role in your homestay.

EVALUATING YOUR STUDENT'S READINESS

First things first, parents: *Is your son or daughter ready for youth exchange?* Consider these factors before you decide:

1. *Age:* Generally, exchange programs have been designed for students in high school (ages 14–18). Children ages 13 and younger will fare better traveling with groups or your entire family, rather than staying with a host family. Students older than 18 will want to investigate study-abroad options at their college or university, particularly those which feature a homestay component.

2. *Maturity level:* More telling than age, however, is your child's maturity. Does your teenager grasp fully the idea of living in another country, with a new family, for an extended period of time? Has he shown interest in youth exchange or other countries before, or is this idea a passing fancy? Can she sit down and discuss the whole idea of going abroad—especially the possibility of culture shock or other difficulties—or does she seem caught up in the romance of living in France for a year? Has he shown the self-control and self-confidence necessary for a successful exchange?

3. *Adaptability:* As much as maturity, the successful exchange student must have the ability to adapt, quickly and completely, to new circumstances. When your family has moved in the past, or when everyone has gone through the upheavals of a difficult divorce, how has your teenager handled the stress and uncertainty resulting from the changes? No one suggests that he must handle every pressure without showing emotion or concern; however, he should demonstrate some ability to focus on the problems involved, deal with them as much as possible, and maintain a strong self-image.

4. *Language skills:* Being completely immersed in another culture will afford your child the best chance to begin acquiring a real fluency in another language. More than any series of books and tapes, the challenge of trying to communicate in everyday matters will yield remarkable returns, even for students who have had no formal language training. Along these lines, consider how your child learns. Does she grasp new concepts quickly, or will she need to develop the patience necessary for learning a new language "on the go?" In some countries—particularly areas whose languages are commonly taught in American high schools, such as France or Spain—students may be required to show a knowledge of the

language before going on exchange. If this rule applies in your child's program, will he have had the requisite classes or years of training?

5. *Level of family support:* Most important, can your child count on the support and encouragement of his family? If you anticipate moving to a new city, going through a divorce, or having other major concerns on your mind during the exchange, will you be able to invest yourself fully in your teenager's exchange experience? Although you will not be physically present during the exchange, your child will catch on quickly if there are major problems at home.

Consider carefully your own motives for the exchange. Do you really embrace the idea of sending your son or daughter on a life-changing experience—or is the trip a convenient way to "farm out" one of your responsibilities? That seems a cruel question, but nothing appears sadder than a student whose parents saw the homestay as a type of boarding school.

Above all, *talk with your son or daughter*. When you hear, straight from his or her own lips, the genuine desire to spend time in another country on a homestay exchange, then you will be ready to proceed.

PLANNING THE EXCHANGE

Once you have passed the hurdles and decided that your family and your teenager are ready for the exchange experience, work together to lay plans for the trip.

1. *Choose a reputable exchange organization.* Using the guidelines outlined earlier, exhaust every avenue to decide which exchange group will provide your child the best homestay experience possible. Consult the directory in this book, which includes 50 exchange programs. Look at these factors closely:

> The organization's stated mission
> Its reputation and history
> The selection process for exchange students and host families
> Its finances and operations
> Its organizational structure and the quality and qualifications of its staff
> The fees, insurance, and other financial requirements for students and host families

2. *Help your child prepare for the selection process.* Depending on the group, the exchange application forms could ask for information ranging from health records to your family's income and expenses (for financial-aid purposes). Complete the forms with your teenager, and explain other difficult portions of the process (such as essay questions, which your child should answer alone). Some companies require interviews with the student or the entire family. Talk through possible questions and answers with your teenager; not only will everyone be thoroughly prepared, but you will also have another chance to gauge your child's potential and commitment as an exchange student. Finally, if pictures, physical examinations, and other requirements must be satisfied, take care of them in plenty of time to avoid unforeseen problems.

3. *Help your son or daughter choose the host country.* Once your student has been accepted by the exchange organization, another decision must be made: In which country will she spend her exchange? If your family's choice of annual vacation spots brings heated arguments, even more care should be invested in the selection of a host country. Think about your child's interests, language training, career goals, family ancestry, hobbies—any facet of his personality that might influence his decision. Research the top choices at the library, and talk to exchange representatives about the relative strengths and weaknesses of each country's program. In the end, step back and let your child make the final decision; although you are paying for the trip, she will be the one living with the decision. In the end, it is the *exchange experience*, not the country, which matters more.

4. *Work with your student to make plans for departure.* Between the confirmation of the host country and family and that fateful trip to the airport, several challenges remain:

- **Language training.** Regardless of her prior language skills, your teenager should make every effort to gain some command of her host language—greetings and family names, at least. Use tapes and other resources available in the library or area bookstores.

- **Shopping and packing.** Once you know where your child is headed, you will know what things he should take for the exchange. (Most groups will provide suggested packing lists; if not, use the list provided in Chapter Three and add to it as you see fit.)

  One firm rule: Do not feel pressured to buy a completely new wardrobe or set of luggage for your student. Instead, shop only for gaps in the list and for items like toiletries and film.

FINANCING THE EXCHANGE

Regardless of whether your teenager's exchange organization is non-profit or for-profit in nature, it does not run its programs on good intentions alone. The trip will cost anywhere from $1,500 for a summer stay and $3,000 for a semester to more than $4,000 for a year (plus spending money and other incidentals). While your organization will economize where possible, you will still pay a good amount of money for the trip.

Before you begin looking for money to pay for the exchange, make sure you understand your financial obligations exactly. What does the basic program fee cover—and what major expenses must still be paid? How much spending money is recommended? What will insurance cost?

You understand the great value of the homestay, as a milestone in your child's life; now, how will you pay for it? You can begin by beating these bushes for money:

Your exchange group's scholarships and loans. Almost every organization offers some type of financial aid for its students, from partial scholarships and installment payment plans to full grants funded by major companies and foreign governments. Once you have settled on an exchange organization, talk frankly with its representatives about the help they can offer.

Community groups. In many areas, local organizations (Rotary, Elks, Lions, Kiwanis, Jaycees, social clubs, and others) sponsor students who participate in youth exchange programs. While their support may be small, every bit helps in financing the homestay. In return for the group's help, your student should plan to make a presentation at a future meeting, describing his homestay experiences.

Your employer. Many corporations have set up scholarships or matching fund programs for their employees' children who are going on exchange. Check with your personnel office for details.

Sources of college money (savings, graduation and birthday gifts, summer job earnings). Because the exchange will have an enormous educational impact on your teenager—opening her eyes to the world, and teaching her adaptability and responsibility—consider tapping your college accounts, particularly if they are in good shape. You would not do this lightly, but the exchange experience should be a clear exception to the "Don't-ever-touch-this-money" rule.

SHARING THE EXCHANGE

Do you feel cheated, knowing that you can share in the planning of (and paying for) the exchange—but not the actual excitement of going on exchange?

Actually, you *can* experience the exchange, through your teenager. Here are some suggestions:

1. *Expand your knowledge about your student's host country and culture.* Work with your child as he researches the background of the culture in which he will be living. Cook a traditional meal using recipes from the host country. Set aside time each week when family members will attempt to talk in that language. Together, improve your understanding of the new environment in which your child will spend her exchange.

2. *Cement your friendship with the host family.* When your teenager learns about his host family, and he writes an introductory letter to them, include a note from you thanking them for their generosity and hospitality. (Taking on a new family member can be no mean feat!) Send along pictures of your family, pets, your home, the neighborhood—any shots that will communicate something about your family and its lifestyle.

3. *Help your teenager to survive the adjustment process.* First, you must gain a thorough understanding of the stages through which your teenager will pass while on exchange. With this knowledge, you will react better when she writes home in the midst of culture shock, or when he seems happier than he ever was at home. Because you know that these stages are normal, your student will draw upon your confidence and understanding for support.

4. *Communicate often—but don't overdo it.* Letters sent weekly or biweekly will allow you to keep in touch without distracting from the exchange experience. From your side, you can share local and family news and offer encouragement and advice; from her side, she can tell stories about her host family, her neighborhood, her school activities, her new friends—all the things that will bring home to you the magic of her exchange. Refrain from frequent

telephone calls, however. Not only are they prohibitively expensive, but they also lead to an unwelcome dependence by your teenager on the calls, disrupting the atmosphere of the homestay. How can your child immerse himself in his host culture when he hears your familiar voice for several hours each week? For the same reasons, you should not plan any visits to the host country during your child's stay.

ASSISTING WITH REENTRY

I experienced two trips and two experiences abroad. One was in Japan; the other was going home. The first trip influenced me. The second influenced everyone around me.

—U.S. student to Japan

When your teenager returns home, he or she will come back a changed person: more mature, full of self-assurance, much more worldly than you remember. Accompanying these positive results, however, will be a number of new pressures:

- Your teenager has gone from being the center of attention to just being "one of the family."

- Just as he became accustomed to a brand-new set of rules, he will be forced to adjust again to the standard procedures of his American life.

- She may feel alienated or behind the times, because she missed significant family or community events during her homestay.

- Because it is easy to glorify one's lifestyle away from home, the return may have shattered those romantic notions he held about "home sweet home."

- Most critically, *your teenager has changed*. He will probably have a deeper appreciation for the world and its different cultures, a more developed sense of tolerance and adaptability, and other skills lacking in his peers.

Not surprisingly, then, your first task will be to make the readjustment as painless as possible. After the first hurrah of welcomes, give your teenager a few days of complete rest and relaxation. She can unpack her things, recover from jet lag and time changes, and begin to develop perspective on her experiences.

Don't try to pull every story out of your child in the first week home! Follow her cues, and listen closely to every episode she relates to you. Look at the photo albums and souvenirs brought back. So many things have happened during the exchange, however, that your student may remember incidents months after her return. Take these things in stride, and talk with your student about the exchange as she develops perspective on it.

During the readjustment process, try to avoid expressing strong emotions or making judgments until you understand the full context of your teenager's homestay. Remember that her months of living as a "minority" in another culture have probably erased many preconceived notions she had about her host country and the world in general. Don't rain on her parade by making crass remarks about raw fish or knickers, when those things might have figured prominently in the memories she cherishes.

Above all, be prepared for symptoms of "reverse culture shock" as your child re-adjusts to his home—but celebrate the special life-changing experiences that he has had. That's the best way you can share fully in the exchange.

9

What About Hosting?

W hat happens if you have now decided that youth exchange is not for you? Or what if finances or school plans force you to reconsider your trip? You can still experience the excitement of exchange—but through the eyes of another person.

Every year, thousands of American families agree to share their homes and lives as hosts for young people from other countries. If you cannot go on exchange yourself—or if you want to continue the experience when you return—hosting an exchange student can be the next best thing to being there.

In black-and-white terms, *why should you consider hosting?*

- You want to learn more about the world—especially the culture of another country—through the perceptions and reactions of a student from that nation.

- You want to share the richness and variety of American culture with a young person from another country. These experiences will contribute greatly to the development of that student's outlook and values.

- In the process, as *your* outlook and values change as a result of your hosting experiences, your family will widen its own horizons and grow closer together.

If these rosy descriptions make hosting sound like a year with the Bradys or the Huxtables, don't be fooled: Hosting an exchange student from another country can be exhausting and frustrating. Mixed with strong doses of love and patience, however, it can also be exhilarating and rewarding.

IS HOSTING RIGHT FOR YOU?

Just like the potential exchange student, every family considering a turn at hosting an exchange student should start with serious thought and discussion. Carefully considering the pros and cons of hosting will yield a realistic picture of how you might react to living with an international student—and, perhaps, prevent that teenager and you many headaches and heartaches later. "When an exchange goes well, it's great; when it turns bad, it's awful," observed one host father.

Begin your "family council" by running through this checklist of questions:

1. Deep down, *what are your primary reasons for hosting a student?* Becoming a host family for the wrong reasons—to provide a sibling for an only child or a live-in babysitter for younger children, to calm tensions within a family, or even to head off a divorce—will quickly lead to disaster.

   Unless you can name at least one strong, positive reason for opening your home to an international student, stop now and save yourself much trouble later.

2. *Will you feel that your home has been "invaded," after a student has lived with you for some time?* How do you react when relatives and friends stay for a few days? Multiply that feeling by months, and gauge your reaction.

   Also, will members of the family become jealous or upset at the constant attention focused on your exchange student? With only so much time for everyone, your guest—really, a new "son" or "daughter," "brother" or "sister"—will demand and receive the affection and support normally reserved for other family members. How will everyone feel?

3. *Will your family's structure and schedule lend themselves to support-ing an exchange student?* Many American homes have both parents working, or a single parent working and caring for the family. While family members have adjusted to taking care of themselves until everyone gets home in the evening, how would an exchange student cope with being a "latchkey kid?" Are there ways in which you can expand your capabilities to deal with those issues (such as having grandparents who live close)?

   Also, if the approaching summer or year already holds plans for a long-awaited family vacation, a major move, or other com-mitments, do not overload circuits by taking on the additional worries of hosting a student.

4. *How will you handle the language barrier?* While you will not be expected to gain fluency in a new language to be an effective host family, you should be willing to learn simple phrases and greetings to welcome your teenager properly. More importantly, will you commit the energy and stamina needed to help your student learn his way around the English language (and others spoken in your home)?

5. *Have you thought through the physical and financial requirements of hosting?* In physical terms, the student should have his own bedroom, or share quarters with enough space for comfort. Also, he will need adequate closet space for his belongings (possibly enough for a year's stay!). In financial terms, you will incur the added expenses of another family member, such as food and transportation around town. Some exchange groups do provide a small stipend to host families to cover these costs, but many organizations steer clear of this practice because it can hamper the development of close relationships between host families and their students. (On the bright side, federal regulations do allow your family a charitable deduction of $50 per month during the ex-change.)

6. *What if the exchange student disagrees strongly with your political, religious, or moral views?* Believe it or not, your student will not embrace American views and beliefs quickly and wholeheartedly. Will you be able to share the heritage and reasoning behind your way of life, then give your student room to make her own decisions? Actually, can you even explain why you do some of the things you do (attend church, vote in elections, have family meetings)?

7. *How involved are you in school and civic affairs?* Can you introduce your exchange student to those activities, so that she can learn from other American families and groups as well as your own?

Next, you should look at the local school system:

1. *Has the school hosted exchange students before?* If so, how have they been treated, and did particular problems arise? What do school officials think about the idea?

2. *In what ways can the school bridge the language barrier?* Are there teachers who are fluent in your student's language? Does the school district have TOEFL-certified (Teachers of English as a Foreign Language) personnel skilled in working with international youth?

3. *Does the school feature a challenging academic curriculum and an active extracurricular program?* Many exchange students—especially those from Western Europe and Japan—will have taken classes that outpace similar offerings in the United States, particularly in the sciences and mathematics. Therefore, to capitalize on their previous work, they must be placed in advanced courses. On the other hand, they could require standard classes in other areas such as English. Can the school take care of these needs? Also, these students participate extensively in extracurricular activities at their home schools; for example, many have after-school club programs ranging form English and judo to chorus and soccer. Will they find a solid range of activities at your school in which they can become involved?

When you are satisfied that your family and the local school are ready for an exchange student, search for answers to the same questions posed in Chapter Three to pick a strong exchange organization:

1. *Who operates the program?*

2. *What are the goals of the program?*

3. *How does the program operate?*

4. *What policies will apply to your student?*

5. *What does the promotional literature reveal about the group?*

6. *What information can be gleaned from other sources* (language teachers, international student advisers, the Council on Standards for International Educational Travel, and the U.S. Information Agency)?

7. *What do other host families and exchange students have to say?*

After you have satisfied your curiosity about the groups in question, request a meeting with area representatives of the programs that interest you the most. Face to face with them, you can evaluate each organization and choose the one that best fits your interests and needs. Here are two areas that will require special scrutiny:

- **Choosing your student.** Does it matter to you that you can pick the nationality, sex, age, and other characteristics of your exchange student? If so, you should ask the area representatives what procedures they follow in assigning students to host families. While some groups do not mind allowing you to pick and choose among incoming students, others believe that they should make assignments themselves (taking into account your preferences). Make sure that you are comfortable with the policy followed by your exchange organization.

- **Covering the expenses of the homestay.** In addition to the basic living expenses incurred by your student, what additional fees will you be assessed by the exchange program? Ideally, you should not pay anything to serve as a host family. Any placement fees or other charges assessed to you should set off warning bells about that particular group. In the same manner, do not be swayed unduly by promises of stipends or living allowances paid to you by a group; such fees are not normally part of a reputable exchange agreement.

Weighing these factors in your decision, you must now come to grips with the question of whether you should host an exchange student in your home for the coming summer, semester, or year. While many resources exist to help you through that period (check the bibliography), the final decision rests with you!

"I've learned that kids are the same the world over," claims Mary Jacobson, who with her husband William ("Bud") has hosted six exchange students in seven years.

The Jacobsons became host parents in 1983 because of their interest in adopting children. When close friends who were also exchange volunteers convinced them that hosting a student would give them good experience with teenagers, "we contacted our local area representative on Tuesday, and on Thursday we picked up our Mexican son from the airport."

Since that year, Bud and Mary have hosted a boy from West Germany, a boy from Switzerland, two girls from Finland, and (most recently) Ian Cruz from the Philippines.

Now that the Jacobsons have adopted two biracial children, Zachary and Joshua, they see hosting as a way to introduce the boys to a broad view of the world. "I want my sons to take people as people even though they may be different," Bud says. "Ian's got a lot of patience," Mary notes, "and he interacts wonderfully with the boys. He just fits in and blends into the family. We're going to miss him an awful lot when he goes back to the Philippines."

"Our sons and daughters have added another dimension to our lives," Mary says. "It's so easy for us to get into our own little rut, thinking that this is Elgin, Illinois, and it's the universe. Hosting brings the world a whole lot closer and at the same time expands our horizons, so we realize that there are neat people out there all over the world, not just in Elgin or the United States. It's exciting to know that we're an international family.

"I'd recommend hosting to anybody in any walk of life," Mary concludes. "I think it adds a great new dimension to your family and to yourself as a person."

PART TWO

Directory of Youth Exchange Programs

LIST OF DIRECTORY ENTRIES

1. Academic and Cultural Exchange
2. Adventures in Real Communication
3. AFS Intercultural Programs
4. American Association of Teachers of German
5. American Farm School
6. American Intercultural Student Exchange
7. American International Youth Student Exchange Program
8. American Secondary Schools for International Students and Teachers
9. Amigos de las Americas
10. ASPECT Foundation
11. ASSE International Student Exchange Programs
12. AYUSA International
13. Casa de Espanol Xelaju
14. CDS International
15. Children's International Summer Villages
16. Council on International Educational Exchange—School Partners Abroad
17. Creative Response
18. Cultural Homestay International
19. De France
20. Educational Resource Development Trust
21. Foreign Study League
22. The Foundation for International Understanding
23. Fulbright-Gesellschaft
24. Iberoamerican Cultural Exchange Program
25. Intercambio Internacional de Estudiantes
26. International Christian Youth Exchange
27. International Education Forum
28. International Student Exchange
29. International Travel Study
30. INTRAX—International Training and Exchange
31. The Irish American Cultural Institute
32. Legacy International
33. NACEL Cultural Exchanges
34. National Association of Secondary School Principals, School Partnerships, International
35. National FFA Organization
36. Open Door Student Exchange

37. PACE Institute International
38. People to People High School Student Ambassador Program
39. Phenix International Campuses
40. ProAmerican Educational and Cultural Exchange
41. Rotary International Exchange Programs
42. School Year Abroad
43. Vistas in Education
44. Wo International Center
45. World Educational Services Foundation
46. World Experience
47. World Heritage
48. World Learning
49. Youth Exchange Service
50. Youth for Understanding International Exchange

ACADEMIC AND CULTURAL EXCHANGE

Through its international educational homestays—which allow students to experience other cultures on a day-to-day basis—Academic and Cultural Exchange strengthens relations between the United States and other countries.

Contact: Louise Heath, Co-Director
5445 Kathy Way
Livermore, CA 94550

Telephone: 800/950-4073
510/449-4726

Fax: 510/449-2228

Non-profit corporation (1988)

Destinations: Australia, Belgium, Brazil, Germany, Hungary, Spain, Ukraine

12 students outbound from the United States
12 students inbound to the United States

P R O G R A M   D E S C R I P T I O N S

Semester/Year Program Abroad
U.S. students live with screened host families and attend high school in the host country.

Semester/Year Program in the United States
International students live with screened host families in the United States and attend high school.

ACADEMIC AND CULTURAL EXCHANGE				
Programs	Length of Stay	Ages Served	Approximate Fee	Requirements
Semester/ Year Program Abroad	6 or 10 months	15 to 19	$4,000 (semester) or $4,450 (year), including international transportation and insurance but excluding domestic U.S. transportation	Two years of the host country's language; B- average (2.70 on 4.00 scale) for the year program
Semester/ Year Program in the United States	6 or 10 months	15 to 19	$2,050 (semester) or $2,550 (year), including insurance but excluding transportation; no fee for host families	Two years of the host country's language; B- average (2.70 on 4.00 scale) for the year program

SELECTION PROCESS

Outbound students complete a formal application and undergo a personal interview conducted in their homes by ACE staffers.

Host families of inbound students complete a formal application and undergo a personal interview conducted in their homes by ACE staffers.

SUPPORT SERVICES

ACE requires orientation sessions for participating students to train them in cross-cultural experiences. Students will be assigned local counselors to provide ongoing support; through regularly scheduled activities, ACE counselors will monitor the progress of each student and offer assistance when needed.

ADVENTURES IN REAL COMMUNICATION

Adventures in Real Communication believes that to motivate students to reach proficiency in another language, they must focus on day-to-day communications skills and global classroom experiences. Founded by language teachers, ARC features pre-travel courses, homestays with host families, and planned excursions within the host country with the express goal of helping students achieve a better command of another language.

Contact: Beverly Wattenmaker, President
4162 Giles Road
Chagrin Falls, OH 44022

Telephone: 216/247-4214
Fax: 216/247-1811

For-profit corporation (1984)

Destinations: Bolivia, Costa Rica, France, Germany, Japan, Lithuania, Mexico, Russia, Spain, Ukraine

Numbers of students not available

ADVENTURES IN REAL COMMUNICATION				
Programs	Length of Stay	Ages Served	Approximate Fee	Requirements
Outbound Family Homestays	2 to 4 weeks	11 to 18	$1,500 to $3,200, including transportation	None
Inbound Family Homestays	2 to 4 weeks	12 to 19	$1,500 to $3,200, including transportation; no fee for host families	None
Individual Homestays	2 to 4 weeks	High school students	$1,500 to $3,200, including transportation	2 years of study in the host language, or demonstrated fluency
Inbound School Year Program	10 months	15 to 19	$3,500 to $5,500, excluding transportation; no fee for host families	Proficiency in English
Outbound School Year Program	10 months	16 to 19	$3,500 to $4,500, including transportation	2 years of study in the host language

PROGRAM DESCRIPTIONS

Outbound Family Homestays

U.S. students will be placed with screened host families. During the homestay, they will visit or attend high school. The program begins with a pre-travel course—a series of classroom lessons designed for students and their teachers before they leave. The actual homestay features planned excursions around the host country, including a visit to the capital city. ARC will work with host schools to design independent study curricula for students wanting academic credit for the exchange.

Inbound Family Homestays

International students will live with screened U.S. host families. In some cases, they will attend English classes in the mornings.

Individual Homestays

Customized independent study/homestay programs will be designed for U.S. students, including pre-travel coursework, planned excursions, and attendance at a host school for academic credit.

Inbound School Year Program

International students will live with U.S. host families and attend a local high school. The program includes orientation sessions, manuals, counseling support, and enrichment activities.

Outbound School Year Program

U.S. students will live with host families and attend a local high school. The program includes orientation sessions, manuals, counseling support, and enrichment activities.

SELECTION PROCESS

Outbound students undergo careful screening by ARC staffers. They must demonstrate a fair degree of language proficiency for those programs requiring two years of language study.

Host families of inbound students also undergo a careful screening process, conducted by ARC community coordinators.

SUPPORT SERVICES

ARC programs feature orientation sessions for students, comprehensive manuals, and trained community coordinators and national directors who can provide personal support as needed.

AFS INTERCULTURAL PROGRAMS

AFS is an international, not-for-profit, non-governmental organization that promotes intercultural learning through worldwide exchange programs for students, teachers, and families. Participants in AFS programs gain a more profound cultural understanding of other societies which is essential to the achievement of social justice and lasting peace in a world of diversity.

Also known as AFS International; American Field Services

Contact: Rosemarie Vibar, Program Information Manager
220 E. 42nd St., Third Floor
New York, NY 10017

Telephone: 800/AFS-INFO
212/949-4242
Fax: 212/949-9379

Non-profit corporation (1947)

Destinations: Argentina, Australia, Austria, Belgium, Bolivia, Brazil, Canada, Chile, Colombia, Costa Rica, Czech Republic, Denmark, Dominican Republic, Eastern Caribbean (Antigua, Barbados, Grenada, St. Lucia, St. Vincent), Ecuador,

Egypt, Finland, France, Germany, Ghana, Guatemala, Honduras, Hong Kong, Hungary, Iceland, Indonesia, Italy, Jamaica, Japan, Kazakhstan, Korea, Latvia, Malaysia, Mexico, Netherlands, New Zealand, Norway, Panama, Paraguay, People's Republic of China, Peru, Portugal, Puerto Rico, Russia, Slovakia, Spain, Sweden, Switzerland, Thailand, Turkey, United Kingdom, Venezuela, Yugoslavia

2,500 students outbound from the United States
3,000 students inbound to the United States

PROGRAM DESCRIPTIONS

Year Homestay Program
U.S. students travel overseas for 11 months to live with a host family and attend high school. AFS staffers and volunteers organize special events during the homestay.

Semester Homestay Program
U.S. students live with a host family and attend high school for five to seven months. AFS staffers and volunteers organize special events during the homestay.

AFS INTERCULTURAL PROGRAMS				
Programs	Length of Stay	Ages Served	Approximate Fee	Requirements
Year Homestay	11 months	15 to 19	$4,995 to $5,395, including international transportation and insurance	None
Semester Homestay	5 to 7 months	15 to 19	$3,995 to $4,495, including international transportation and insurance	None
Summer & Winter Homestay	4 weeks (winter); 6 to 10 weeks (summer)	15 to 19	$2,295 to $3,395, including international transportation and insurance	None
Team Missions Programs	3 weeks	15 to 18 (16 to 18 for the "peace care" program)	$2,845 to $3,395, including international transportation and insurance	Students in the "peace care" program must demonstrate a prior knowledge of French.
Year Hosting	1 academic year	15 to 18	Cost varies from country to country; no fee for host families	None
Summer Hosting	3 to 4 weeks	15 to 20	Cost varies from country to country; no fees for host families	None

Summer and Winter Homestay Programs

For a shorter stay abroad, AFS offers six- to 10- week summer programs and four-week winter programs.

AFS winter departures to Costa Rica or France will include either a homestay or a homestay combined with intensive language study.

AFS summer departures feature these options: homestay only; homestay combined with language training in Spanish, French, German, Italian, or Japanese; homestay with an "outdoor education" component in Australia, New Zealand, the Netherlands, or Switzerland; or homestay with an "environmental studies" component in Brazil.

Team Mission Program

The Team Missions Program takes groups of 30 students and four experienced teachers on three-week programs to selected countries. The trip combines study tours, hands-on involvement in volunteer projects and (in some cases) homestays in the following topic areas: the global economy, democratic traditions, "peace care," environmental studies, and cultural studies.

Year Hosting

International students live with screened U.S. host families and attend high school for one academic year.

Summer Hosting

International students live with screened U.S. host families after taking intensive English language training on a university campus.

SELECTION PROCESS

Outbound students complete a comprehensive application form (with short essay questions and teacher recommendations), medical report, and school transcripts. Also required is a personal interview with a local AFS volunteer.

The application deadline for winter departures is November 15. The application deadline for summer departures is March 15. The application deadline for Team Missions Programs is April 1.

AFS offers several financial assistance programs: *merit awards* for students with excellent academic and leadership records; *designated scholarship awards* for students from specific states or with certain interests; *country-specific* scholarships for students going to Mexico, Germany, or Japan; *corporate scholarships* for students whose parents are employees of designated companies; and *general grants* for students demonstrating true financial need. Full details will be included in the AFS application packet.

Host families of inbound students complete a formal application and a personal interview with a local AFS volunteer. Early applications are encouraged, but most deadlines are flexible. Host families will be allowed to review the files of inbound students and express their preferences for individual students.

SUPPORT SERVICES

AFS support services include comprehensive pre-departure orientations, arrival orientations in the host country, and continuous support throughout the exchange from trained local volunteers. Flight chaperones accompany students to the host country.

AMERICAN ASSOCIATION OF TEACHERS OF GERMAN

Living and studying in Germany is the basis of the German Summer Study Program sponsored by AATG. The program represents a significant step towards achieving the highest goal of intercultural language education: improved global awareness and understanding.

Contact: Helene Zimmer-Loew, Executive Director
112 Haddontowne Court, #104
Cherry Hill, NJ 08034

Telephone: 609/795-5553
Fax: 609/795-9398

Non-profit corporation (1947)

Destinations: Germany

90 students outbound from the United States

AMERICAN ASSOCIATION OF TEACHERS OF GERMAN				
Programs	Length of Stay	Ages Served	Approximate Fee	Requirements
German Summer Study Program	4 weeks	15 to 18	$1,995, including international transportation and a blanket insurance policy	At least 2 years of German language study and the recommendation of their instructor

PROGRAM DESCRIPTIONS

German Summer Study Program

U.S. students live with German host families in the summer. They attend classes in a local *gymnasium* (high school). Field trips will be coordinated by a U.S. teacher accompanying the group of exchange students.

SELECTION PROCESS

Outbound students complete an application form, a *personalbogen* (application form in German), a parental consent form, and a confidential teacher's recommendation. The application deadline for the summer program is March 1.

SUPPORT SERVICES

On-site counseling is provided by the U.S. teacher accompanying each group of students, as well as staffers of the Pedagogical Exchange Service (an agency of the German government).

AMERICAN FARM SCHOOL

Greek Summer is a six-week program of cultural exchange and personal discovery. U.S. high school students are given an opportunity to work on a much-needed project (such as building a road) in a Greek village, to live with a Greek family, and to see some of the glories of Greece.

Contact: Patricia Mulhern, Program Coordinator
1133 Broadway
New York, NY 10010

Telephone: 212/463-8434
Fax: 212/463-8208

Non-profit corporation (1970)

Destinations: Greece

40 students outbound from the United States

AMERICAN FARM SCHOOL				
Programs	Length of Stay	Ages Served	Approximate Fee	Requirements
Greek Summer	6 weeks	Grades 10–12	$1,950, excluding transportation	None

PROGRAM DESCRIPTIONS

Greek Summer

A group of 40 U.S. students live with selected host families in a small village in Greece and complete a work project that benefits the villagers. Also, the students participate in activities at the American Farm School in Thessaloniki and a nine-day excursion throughout Greece.

SELECTION PROCESS

Outbound students submit an application form (including three essays) and letters of recommendation and participate in an interview. Early applications are strongly recommended.

Once accepted, students must complete a medical information form and a parental release form.

American Farm School offers one complete scholarship sponsored by its alumni society, with additional awards possible. Students must request an application for the scholarship to be considered.

SUPPORT SERVICES

Students participate in a three-day orientation session upon arriving in Greece. Three professional staffers and four trained counselors supervise students during the exchange.

AMERICAN INTERCULTURAL STUDENT EXCHANGE

AISE is a non-profit educational foundation founded for the purpose of fostering better international understanding and appreciation through language and cultural exchange. AISE believes that international student exchange offers students, their parents, and host families an irreplaceable opportunity to deepen their comprehension and respect of other peoples and cultures.

Contact: Klaus Bergmann, Director of Programs
7720 Herschel Avenue
La Jolla, CA 92037

Telephone: 800/SIBLING
619/459-9761
Fax: 619/459-5301

Non-profit corporation (1980)

Destinations: Australia, Austria, Belgium, Brazil, Colombia, Czech Republic, Denmark, Ecuador, Finland, France, Germany, Hungary, Italy, Japan, Korea, Netherlands, New Zealand, Norway, Peru, Poland, Spain, Sweden, Switzerland, Thailand, Turkey, Yugoslavia

350 students outbound from the United States
3,100 students inbound to the United States

AMERICAN INTERCULTURAL STUDENT EXCHANGE				
Programs	Length of Stay	Ages Served	Approximate Fee	Requirements
School Year Abroad Program	1 academic year	15 to 18	$4,600 for nations in western Europe and $4,900 for Australia, including transportation	At least a 2.70 grade-point average (on a 4.00 scale); 2 years of language study for France, Germany, Spain, and Switzerland
Semester Abroad Program	1 semester	15 to 18	$4,700, including transportation	At least a 2.70 grade-point average
8-Week Summer Homestay to Australia	1 semester	15 to 18	$3,300, including transportation	None
Summer Abroad Program	5 weeks	15 to 18	$2,505, including transportation	None
5-Week Summer Language and Homestay Program	5 weeks	15 to 18	$3,200, including transportation	None
School Year Program in America	1 academic year	15 to 18	$4,450, including transportation and insurance; no fees for host families	A good command of the English language
Summer Homestay Program in America	5 weeks	15 to 18	$2,067, including transportation and insurance; no fees for host families	None

PROGRAM DESCRIPTIONS

School Year Abroad Program
U.S. students live with screened host families and attend high school.

Semester Abroad Program
U.S. students live with screened host families and attend high school.

Eight-Week Summer Homestay to Australia
U.S. students live with screened Australian host families and attend classes in local high schools.

Summer Abroad Program
U.S. students live with screened host families in Denmark, France, Germany, Italy, Norway, Spain, or Sweden.

Five-Week Summer Language and Homestay Program
U.S. students live with screened host families in France or Spain; at the same time, they participate in an intensive language study program with three-hour classes for five days each week.

School Year Program in America
International students live with screened U.S. host families and attend high school classes.

Summer Homestay Program in America
International students live with screened U.S. host families.

SELECTION PROCESS

Outbound students must complete an application form (with a personal essay) and supply a health certificate, school transcript, and recommendations from the student's principal and teachers. Also, AISE requires a personal interview. Students are selected on the basis of character, grade-point average, personal essay, and recommendations.

The deadline for most AISE programs is April 1.

Host families of inbound students undergo a preliminary telephone interview. Beyond this step, AISE requires a home interview, application form, and three references.

SUPPORT SERVICES

AISE provides pre-departure and post-arrival orientation sessions for most programs. For counseling support, AISE relies upon its network of 15 regional offices, which oversee more than 1,000 area representatives.

AMERICAN INTERNATIONAL YOUTH STUDENT EXCHANGE PROGRAM

AIYSEP facilitates exchange programs for high school students based on the philosophy that a greater international understanding is accomplished among people of the world through cultural and homestay programs. Its goal is to promote unity, peace, and understanding by offering qualified students the opportunity to spend a school year, a semester, or a summer with a host family in another country.

Contact: Francella T. Hall, Executive Director
4340 Redwood Highway
San Rafael, CA 94903

Telephone: 800/347-7575
415/435-4049
Fax: 415/499-5651

Non-profit corporation (1980)

Destinations: Australia, Austria, Belgium, Brazil, Canada, Chile, Croatia, Czech Republic, Denmark, Finland, France, Germany, Ireland, Italy, Japan, Netherlands, New Zealand, Norway, Portugal, Spain, Sweden, Switzerland, United Kingdom

100 students outbound from the United States
150 students inbound to the United States

PROGRAM DESCRIPTIONS

Year/Semester Program Abroad
U.S. students live with screened host families and attend classes in a local high school.

Summer Program Abroad
U.S. students live with screened host families and participate in language classes.

Year/Semester Program in the United States
International students live with screened U.S. host families and attend high school.

Summer Program to the United States
International students live with screened U.S. host families and participate in language classes.

SELECTION PROCESS

Outbound students must complete an application form (including essays) and supply a school transcript, medical examination and release, and teacher recommendations. Also, students must be interviewed by an AIYSEP counselor.

AIYSEP offers full, half, and partial scholarships for qualified students. Contact AIYSEP for application forms.

Host families of inbound students will be interviewed by an AIYSEP counselor. Also, the family must complete a host family application form and submit references. The principal of the local school must sign an agreement to accept the exchange student in classes.

SUPPORT SERVICES

AIYSEP students attend orientation sessions before they leave; once they arrive in the host country, they participate in a second session. They and their host families receive comprehensive manuals for further reference. Trained local counselors offer additional support.

AMERICAN INTERNATIONAL YOUTH STUDENT EXCHANGE PROGRAM				
Programs	Length of Stay	Ages Served	Approximate Fee	Requirements
Year/ Semester Program Abroad	1 semester or academic year	15 to 19	$2,995 to $3,595 (semester) or $3,395 to $4,195 (year), including transportation and insurance	3 years of studying the host language; 2.70 grade-point average (on 4.00 scale)
Summer Program Abroad	4, 6, or 8 weeks	14 to 19	$2,800, including transportation and insurance	2.70 grade-point average (on 4.00 scale)
Year/ Semester Program in the United States	1 semester or academic year	15 to 17	$2,000 to $2,195 (semester) or $2,595 (year), including insurance but excluding transportation; no fee for host families	A good command of the English language
Summer Program to the United States	4, 6, or 8 weeks	14 to 19	$895 to $1,600, including insurance but excluding transportation; no fee for host families	None

AMERICAN SECONDARY SCHOOLS FOR INTERNATIONAL STUDENTS AND TEACHERS

ASSIST—an association of independent secondary schools—provides cross-cultural experiences for young people from around the world to spend one year as a student ambassador in selected boarding and day schools. Competition for ASSIST programs is very strong.

Contact: Kenneth I. Lindfors, President
40 General Miller Road
Peterborough, NH 03458

Telephone: 603/924-9659
Fax: 603/924-3767

Non-profit corporation (1969)

Destinations: Australia, Belgium, Bulgaria, Denmark, Germany, Hungary, India, Latvia, Lithuania, Romania, Spain, Sweden

15 students outbound from the United States
139 students inbound to the United States

P R O G R A M   D E S C R I P T I O N S

Outbound Program—Australia and Spain
Two independent schools in Australia and one school in Spain offer full grants to U.S. students from ASSIST-affiliated schools to live with host families and attend classes.

Outbound Program—Germany
U.S. students from ASSIST-affiliated schools live with a German host family and attend classes in the local *gymnasium*.

Inbound Program
International students serve as student ambassadors in ASSIST-affiliated schools. They receive scholarships for participating in the program.

Traveling Seminar—21st Century Europe
U.S. students from ASSIST-affiliated schools travel as a group to Europe for a traveling seminar. They visit sites in Germany and

AMERICAN SECONDARY SCHOOLS FOR INTERNATIONAL STUDENTS AND TEACHERS				
Programs	Length of Stay	Ages Served	Approximate Fee	Requirements
Outbound Program— Australia and Spain	1 academic year	15 to 18	$2,000, excluding transportation and insurance	None
Outbound Program— Germany	1 academic year	15 to 18	$2,800, excluding transportation and insurance	None
Inbound Program	1 academic year	15 to 18	$0 to $11,975 (depending upon the scholarship offered), excluding transportation and insurance	None
Traveling Seminar— 21st Century Europe	2 weeks	High school sophomores and juniors	$1,350, excluding some land transportation expenses and some meals	None

Belgium; while in Germany, they live with the families of former ASSIST exchange students.

SELECTION PROCESS

Outbound students must undergo an extensive screening process, including personal interviews and an evaluation of academic achievement.

SUPPORT SERVICES

ASSIST monitors the progress of its exchange students through the help of its affiliate schools in the United States, Germany, Spain, and Australia.

AMIGOS DE LAS AMERICAS

Through Amigos de las Americas—a private volunteer group affiliated with the Pan American Health Organization—young volunteers gain leadership skills by serving in public health projects in Latin America and the Caribbean. Since 1965, more than 16,000 Amigos volunteers have lived and worked in 15 countries.

Contact: Celdie Sencion, Director of Marketing
5618 Star Lane
Houston, TX 77057

Telephone: 800/231-7796
713/782-5290
Fax: 713/782-9267

Non-profit corporation (1965)

Destinations: Brazil, Costa Rica, Dominican Republic, Ecuador, Honduras, Mexico, Paraguay

600 students outbound from the United States

PROGRAM DESCRIPTIONS

Amigos de las Americas

U.S. students live in homes in a rural community, providing public health services in Latin American and Caribbean countries. Volunteers work in teams in schools, health clinics, and houses.

SELECTION PROCESS

Outbound students must undergo a three- to six-month training program, usually within a local Amigos chapter. The course includes training in Spanish or Portuguese; Latin American history and culture; first aid, public health, and community development; and human relations skills. Students who do not live in a chapter city may complete an independent study program via correspondence.

SUPPORT SERVICES

Before the trip, Amigos chapters raise funds to cover many expenses of the exchange. During the trip, the community's mayor, local doctor, or town priest oversees the Amigos group, and Amigos field staffers visit regularly to deliver supplies and mail.

AMIGOS DE LAS AMERICAS				
Programs	Length of Stay	Ages Served	Approximate Fee	Requirements
Amigos de las Americas	4 to 8 weeks	At least 16 years old	$2,325 to $2,985, including international transportation	Proficiency in Spanish or Portuguese; 3 to 6 months of Amigos training

ASPECT FOUNDATION

ASPECT Foundation—an international educational organization—bridges cultures, builds bonds of international friendship and understanding, and offers a means for culturally enriching and mutually rewarding experiences.

Contact: Janice Haigh, Vice President
26 Third Street
San Francisco, CA 94103

Telephone: 415/777-4348
Fax: 415/777-0907

Non-profit corporation (1985)

Destinations: Argentina, Austria, Belgium, Brazil, Canary Islands, Colombia, Czech Republic, Denmark, Ecuador, Finland, France, Germany, Indonesia, Italy, Japan, Korea, Mexico, Netherlands, Norway, Paraguay, Poland, Russia, Spain, Sweden, Switzerland, United Kingdom, Yugoslavia

1 student outbound from the United States
2,580 students inbound to the United States

ASPECT FOUNDATION				
Programs	Length of Stay	Ages Served	Approximate Fee	Requirements
Short-Term/ Semester/ School Year Abroad	Several weeks, a semester, or an academic year	High school age	$2,000 to $5,500, including transportation but excluding insurance	At least 1 year of foreign language study (for Japan, a working knowledge of Japanese)
Academic Year Program	1 semester or academic year	15 to 19	$4,000 to $6,000, including transportation; a 2- to 3-week preparatory course is available at an additional cost.	English language proficiency
Short-Term Cultural Homestay	2 to 8 weeks	14 to 21	$1,200 to $1,700, excluding transportation	None
Boarding School Program in the United States	1 or more academic years	14 to 18	$10,000 to $28,000 (depending upon the school selected), including tuition, room and board, international transportation and insurance	None

PROGRAM DESCRIPTIONS

Short-Term/Semester/School Year Abroad
U.S. students travel to one of four countries to live with screened host families. During the semester or year program, each student attends high school.

Academic Year Program
International students live with screened U.S. host families while attending school.

Short-Term Cultural Homestay
International students take part in a two- to eight-week cultural homestay in the United States. Local coordinators organize and supervise programs to expose students to American culture.

Boarding School Program in the United States
International students study and live at a U.S. boarding school. During the year, ASPECT staffers maintain contact with the students. Participating schools must demonstrate experience with international students, strong academic curricula, and a wide array of extracurricular activities.

SELECTION PROCESS

Outbound students must complete an application form and undergo a personal interview. In addition, they must submit proof of at least one year of foreign language study.

Host families of inbound students must complete an application form and undergo a family interview.

SUPPORT SERVICES

In addition to pre-departure and post-arrival orientation sessions, ASPECT provides ongoing counseling support through its four regional offices and a network of more than 400 area representatives. Certain programs also feature preparatory training in language and customs.

ASSE INTERNATIONAL STUDENT EXCHANGE PROGRAMS

Founded by the Swedish government as the American Scandinavian Student Exchange, ASSE facilitates students exchanges between the United States and Scandinavia. Its programs now include Australia, Canada, Mexico, New Zealand, Japan, and 16 nations in Europe. ASSE is affiliated with the worldwide Sons of Norway organization.

Contact: Admissions
228 North Coast Highway
Laguna Beach, CA 92651

Telephone: 714/494-4100
Fax: 714/497-8704

Non-profit corporation (1976)

Destinations: Australia, Canada, Czech Republic, Denmark, Estonia, Finland, France, Germany, Iceland, Italy, Japan, Mexico, Netherlands, New Zealand, Norway, Portugal, Poland, Spain, Sweden, Switzerland, United Kingdom

Numbers of students not available

PROGRAM DESCRIPTIONS

Academic Year Abroad
U.S. students live with host families and attend school in another country. While no prior language instruction is required, the post-arrival orientation includes 10 to 14 days of intensive language and cultural training.

Summer Homestay Program
U.S. students live with host families in another country. Orientation and counseling support are included.

Summer Language Study Homestay
U.S. students traveling to France, Germany, or Spain may choose a language study homestay, with instruction in small groups according to language ability.

Young Ambassadors' Program to Russia
U.S. students spend 11 days on an educational study tour of Russia, including visits to Moscow, Minsk, and St. Petersburg. The trip features social meetings with Russian youth.

ASSE INTERNATIONAL STUDENT EXCHANGE PROGRAMS				
Programs	Length of Stay	Ages Served	Approximate Fee	Requirements
Academic Year Abroad	10 months	15 to 18	$2,600 to $6,250, including transportation (except for U.S./Canada exchanges) and insurance	None
Summer Homestay Program	6 weeks	15 to 18	$2,200 to $2,300, including transportation and insurance	None
Summer Language Study Homestay	4 weeks	15 to 18	$2,600, including transportation, insurance, and excursions	None
Young Ambassadors' Program to Russia	11 days	15 to 18	$2,150, including escort, transportation, accommodations, and insurance	None
Academic Year or Semester in North America	Academic year or semester	15 to 18	$2,600 to $5,500, including transportation and insurance; no fee for host families	None
Summer in the United States	4 weeks	15 to 18	$1,950 to $2,100, including transportation and insurance; no fee for host families	None

Academic Year or Semester in North America

International students live with U.S. host families and attend high school. Orientation and local counseling support are provided.

Summer in the United States

International students spend four weeks in a language study homestay with U.S. host families. The program includes planned excursions, orientations, and counseling support.

SELECTION PROCESS

Outbound students and *host families of inbound students* undergo a thorough screening process by ASSE staffers and school personnel.

SUPPORT SERVICES

ASSE representatives conduct pre-departure and post-arrival orientation sessions for students and host families. Also, they offer local counseling support as appropriate.

AYUSA INTERNATIONAL

AYUSA International sponsors international educational exchange programs for high school students.

Contact: Rebecca Megerssa, Director of Program Development
One Post Street, Suite 700
San Francisco, CA 94104

Telephone: 415/434-1212
Fax: 415/986-4620

Non-profit corporation (1980)

Destinations: Australia, Baltic States, Belgium, Brazil, Bulgaria, Colombia, Commonwealth of Independent States, Croatia, Czech Republic, Denmark, France, Germany, Hungary, Italy, Japan, Macedonia, Mexico, Netherlands, New Zealand, Poland, Romania, Slovakia, Slovenia, Spain, Sweden, Switzerland, Thailand, United Kingdom, Yugoslavia

50 students outbound from the United States
1,400 students inbound to the United States

PROGRAM DESCRIPTIONS

AYUSA Study Abroad
U.S. students live with screened host families and attend high school.

AYUSA INTERNATIONAL				
Programs	Length of Stay	Ages Served	Approximate Fee	Requirements
AYUSA Study Abroad	A summer, semester, or academic year	15 to 18	$1,895 to $4,995, including insurance but excluding transportation	2 years of language training (for the semester and year programs)
Academic Year in the United States	1 summer, semester, or academic year	15 to 18	$3,500 to $5,000, including transportation and insurance; no fee for host families	Demonstrated proficiency in the English language
Semester in the United States	1 semester	15 to 18	$2,500 to $4,000, including transportation and insurance; no fee for host families	Demonstrated proficiency in the English language

Academic Year in the United States

International students live with screened U.S. host families and attend high school.

Semester in the United States

International students live with screened U.S. host families and attend high school.

SELECTION PROCESS

Outbound students must have at least a "C" academic average and show evidence of maturity and adaptability.

Host families of inbound students will be screened by AYUSA staffers. They must complete a family interview and submit references.

SUPPORT SERVICES

Beyond the standard pre-departure and post-arrival orientation sessions, AYUSA employs a network of community counselors who serve as liaisons for students, host families, host schools, and AYUSA headquarters. They submit regular progress reports which are forwarded to overseas sponsors and parents.

CASA DE ESPANOL XELAJU

Casa de Espanol Xelaju seeks to offer students top-quality Spanish language instruction while presenting them with a comprehensive view of Guatemalan life. This is achieved through close contact with Guatemalan instructors and families, as well as other activities that teach them about Guatemalan history, culture, and society.

Contact: Julio Batres, Founder
1022 St. Paul Avenue
St. Paul, MN 55116

Telephone: 612/690-9471
Fax: 612/690-9471

Non-profit corporation (1983)

Destinations: Guatemala

600 students outbound from the United States

CASA DE ESPANOL XELAJU				
Programs	Length of Stay	Ages Served	Approximate Fee	Requirements
Casa de Espanol Xelaju	1 to 4 weeks	High school students and older	$150 per week, excluding transportation and insurance	None

PROGRAM DESCRIPTIONS

Casa de Espanol Xelaju

U.S. students travel to Guatemala for professional instruction in Spanish, while living with Guatemalan families.

SELECTION PROCESS

Outbound students must complete an application form.

SUPPORT SERVICES

Students participate in orientation sessions upon arriving in Guatemala. Bilingual counselors and professors can offer personal support to students.

CDS INTERNATIONAL

A non-profit organization dedicated to promoting international awareness in business and education, CDS International provides unique opportunities for professionals and students to gain practical training in the global marketplace. The organization's extensive network of international contacts and professional staff enable it to offer a diversified portfolio of exchanges and training programs designed to prepare individuals for an increasingly competitive international market.

Also known as The Carl Duisberg Society

Contact: Wolfgang Linz, Executive Director
330 Seventh Avenue, 19th Floor
New York, NY 10001-5010

Telephone: 212/760-1400
Fax: 212/268-1288

Non-profit corporation (1968)

Destinations: Germany

Numbers of students not available

CDS INTERNATIONAL				
Programs	Length of Stay	Ages Served	Approximate Fee	Requirements
Congress-Bundestag Youth Exchange	1 year	18 to 24	The U.S. Congress and the German parliament cover all costs of the program for each student, with the exception of compensation paid to host families during the internship portion of the exchange.	A high school diploma with a good academic record; previous knowledge of German not required but strongly recommended.

PROGRAM DESCRIPTIONS

Congress-Bundestag Youth Exchange

U.S. students participate for two months in intensive language training in Germany, followed by four months of classroom training at a German technical school or other institution of higher education. Then, the students will be placed in internships with German firms for five or six months of on-the-job training. The students live with German families or, in some cases, dormitories.

SELECTION PROCESS

Outbound students complete an application form and an interview.

SUPPORT SERVICES

CDS offers orientation sessions, student handbooks, trained counselors and professional staffers in the host country.

CHILDREN'S INTERNATIONAL SUMMER VILLAGES

Founded by psychologist Doris Twitchell Allen, Children's International Summer Villages provides multinational summer camps tailored to the interests and abilities of targeted age groups.

Contact: Sally Stein, Administrative Secretary
833 N. Dorset Road
Troy, OH 45373

Telephone: 513/335-4640
Fax: 513/335-4640

Non-profit corporation (1950)

Destinations: Argentina, Australia, Austria, Belgium, Brazil, Bulgaria, Canada, Chile, Costa Rica, Czech Republic, Denmark, Egypt, El Salvador, Faeroe Islands, Finland, France, Germany, Great Britain, Greece, Guatemala, Honduras, Hungary, Iceland, India, Israel, Italy, Japan, Jordan, Korea, Luxembourg, Mexico, Mongolia, Netherlands, New Zealand, Nigeria, Norway, Phillipines, Poland, Portugal, Romania, Russia, Senegal, Sierra Leone, Spain, Sweden, Thailand, Turkey, Uruguay, Yugoslavia

267 students outbound from the United States
276 students inbound from the United States

PROGRAM DESCRIPTIONS

Interchange
Students will be matched according to sex, age, and interest; then, they will take part in reciprocal one-month stays with each other's family. The program includes both group activities and family activities.

Seminar Camp
Students attend a camp to take part in activities designed to help them learn about the ideas and opinions of other cultures around the world. Trained staffers lead the camp sessions, under the aegis of the CISV office in the United Kingdom.

Junior Counselor
Students chosen through local CISV chapters (19 in the United States) undergo a mandatory training session, then serve as assistant counselors during the standard International Summer Village for 11-year-old children from different nations.

CHILDREN'S INTERNATIONAL SUMMER VILLAGES				
Programs	Length of Stay	Ages Served	Approximate Fee	Requirements
Interchange	2 summers	12 to 15	$250 to $500 each summer, excluding transportation	None
Seminar Camp	3 weeks	17 to 18	$250, excluding transportation	None
Junior Counselor	4 weeks	17 to 18	Approximately $250 (varying among local chapters, excluding transportation	None

SELECTION PROCESS

Outbound students undergo careful screening through local CISV chapters. Students aiming for Junior Counselor status must complete a mandatory training program coordinated through the nearest CISV chapter.

Host families of inbound students must undergo a similar application process (and, in the Interchange program, agree to participate for two summers).

SUPPORT SERVICES

Primary support comes from the counseling activities of 63 CISV national associations around the globe. Local chapters in each country coordinate training sessions and provide counseling support as needed.

COUNCIL ON INTERNATIONAL EDUCATIONAL EXCHANGE— SCHOOL PARTNERS ABROAD

CIEE began in 1947 to restore student exchange opportunities after World War II. Its School Partners Abroad program links U.S. schools with counterpart schools in Asia, Europe, and Latin America for year-round educational activities, including an annual reciprocal exchange of students.

Contact: Ellen Lautz, Director of Secondary Education Programs
205 East 42nd Street
New York, NY 10017

Telephone: 212/661-1414
Fax: 212/972-3231

Non-profit corporation (1947)

Destinations: Costa Rica, France, Germany, Japan, Russia, Spain

1,250 students outbound from the United States
1,800 students inbound to the United States

COUNCIL ON INTERNATIONAL EDUCATIONAL EXCHANGE— SCHOOL PARTNERS ABROAD				
Programs	Length of Stay	Ages Served	Approximate Fee	Requirements
School Partners Abroad	3 to 4 weeks	High school students	$700 to $2,000 (depending on the country), including transportation and insurance	None
3-Month Exchange to Germany	3 months	High school students	$1,500, including transportation and insurance	None
Youth in China	1 month	15 to 18	$3,500, including international transportation and insurance	At least 1 semester of Chinese language studies or social studies focusing on China

PROGRAM DESCRIPTIONS

School Partners Abroad

U.S. students travel in groups led by teachers to visit partner schools in a reciprocal exchange. Participants live with host families and attend school; short field trips are also arranged.

Three-Month Exchange to Germany

U.S. and German students who are alumni of the School Partners Abroad program return to their host school for a homestay.

Youth in China

U.S. students participate in summer language classes at a Chinese secondary school and live in a residence hall with Chinese students.

SELECTION PROCESS

Outbound students must complete an application form (including school recommendations) to be screened by CIEE's U.S. office.

Host families of inbound students will be reviewed by overseas CIEE offices, in conjunction with host school officials.

SUPPORT SERVICES

CIEE employs the resources of a network of youth organizations and educational associations to operate its programs. Primary support comes from the educators and community leaders who organize the School Partners Abroad program.

CREATIVE RESPONSE

Creative Response is an educational foundation for youth designed to promote international and intercultural understanding through the arts. A non-profit foundation, Creative Response firmly believes that young people—through their involvement in neighborhood, international, and environmental efforts—can take a leadership role in improving their individual and global communities.

Also known as City at Peace; Voices

Contact: Norma Johnson, Director of Program Development
9502 Lee Highway, Suite B
Fairfax, VA 22031

Telephone: 703/385-4494
Fax: 703/273-6568

Non-profit corporation (1982)

Destinations: Australia, Belgium, Brazil, Byelorus, Canada, Costa Rica, Czech Republic, Georgia, Germany, Hungary, Indonesia, Israel, Japan, Kazakhstan, Korea, Latvia, Netherlands, New Zealand, Nigeria, People's Republic of China, Phillipines, Poland, Russia, South Africa, Ukraine, United Kingdom

200 students outbound from the United States
160 students inbound to the United States

PROGRAM DESCRIPTIONS

Performing Arts Summer Exchanges
U.S. students study theater and prepare a musical built around the themes of international understanding and global awareness. Each group of 15 students live together in a host city as they rehearse the play and present it to local audiences.

Creative Response Domestic Exchanges
U.S. students take part in a summer program within the United States, joining a group of students from up to 30 other countries to learn about environmental issues and global relations.

International Student Leadership Forum
Students from as many as 20 nations engage in performing arts and other activities in a host city. They explore leadership issues, global relations, and cross-cultural communications.

Choral/Orchestra/Drama Group Exchanges

Choruses, theater groups, and youth orchestras travel to other nations to perform before audiences at schools, theaters, and other public places. They combine with similar groups in the host country to plan and perform these concerts.

SELECTION PROCESS

Outbound students must complete an application form, including two recommendations from teachers and conductors and an audition/ interview with Creative Response staffers. Applications must be submitted by Dec. 31 for students to qualify for programs conducted the following year; they will be taken through Jan. 31 if spaces remain open.

A limited number of scholarships are available for qualified students.

Host families of inbound students must complete an application form and be interviewed by host family coordinators. Recommendations from teachers, clergy, or community officials may be requested.

SUPPORT SERVICES

Creative Response offers orientation sessions, cultural preparation materials, and re-entry packets to help students make smooth transitions during the exchange. In addition, interpreters work with student groups during rehearsals (since performances will be done in the local language).

CREATIVE RESPONSE				
Programs	Length of Stay	Ages Served	Approximate Fee	Requirements
Performing Arts Summer Exchanges	4 to 6 weeks	13 to 19	$2,900 to $3,800, including transportation	None
Creative Response Domestic Exchanges	4 to 6 weeks	13 to 19	$1,500, excluding transportation	None
International Student Leadership Forum	2 weeks	13 to 19	$600 to $900, excluding transportation	None
Choral/Orchestra/ Drama Group Exchanges	1 to 3 weeks	13 to 19	$1,300 to $2,800, including transportation (teachers/ conductors travel free)	None

CULTURAL HOMESTAY INTERNATIONAL

Organized in 1980 by the Corporation for Economic Education, Cultural Homestay International focused initially on Japanese inbound students. CHI now sends thousands of students around the world to participate in homestay exchanges—the ideal way to develop friendship and understanding among different cultures.

Also known as Cultural Homestay Institute

Contact: Gayle Peebles, Outbound Manager
1672 Deer Run
Santa Rosa, CA 95405

Telephone: 800/395-2726
415/459-5397
Fax: 415/459-2182

Non-profit corporation (1980)

Destinations: Australia, Austria, Belgium, Brazil, Canada, Colombia, Czech Republic, Denmark, Finland, France, Germany, Ghana, Japan, Netherlands, New Zealand, People's Republic of China, Poland, Reunion, Russia, Spain, Switzerland, Taiwan, Thailand, Yugoslavia

150 students outbound from the United States
6,150 students inbound to the United States

PROGRAM DESCRIPTIONS

Academic Year Program Abroad
Students from North America travel overseas to attend high school and live with a host family.

Group Homestay Abroad
U.S. students or adults travel in groups to other countries to live with host families.

Academic High School Year or Semester in North America
International students live with North American host families and attend high school to develop fluency in English.

CULTURAL HOMESTAY INTERNATIONAL				
Programs	Length of Stay	Ages Served	Approximate Fee	Requirements
Academic Year Program Abroad	1 semester or academic year	15 to 18	$3,350 to $5,500, including transportation	None
Group Homestay Abroad	3 to 6 weeks	At least 15 years old	$1,990 to $2,850, including transportation	None
Academic High School Year or Semester in North America	1 semester or academic year	High school students	$1,625 (semester) or $2,300 to $2,800 (year), excluding transportation	Ability to communicate in English
Group Homestay in North America Program	2 to 5 weeks	High school students	$175 to $200 per week, excluding transportation	None

Group Homestay in North America Program

International students live with host families and attend language and culture classes while participating in educational tours of local communities.

SELECTION PROCESS

Outbound students must complete an application form, submit teacher recommendations and an academic transcript (2.50 GPA or better), and be interviewed by CHI. The deadline is February 1 for the fall semester and July 1 for the spring semester.

Host families of inbound students must complete an application form, submit three references, and be interviewed by CHI. The deadline is May 15 to receive a student the following fall.

SUPPORT SERVICES

More than 720 academic coordinators and teacher coordinators work with individual students during the homestays, providing counseling and advice; also, academic counselors request monthly Academic Program Reports from both students and host parents, to be sent to the student's parents by CHI's professional staff.

Other services include orientation sessions and student handbooks.

DE FRANCE

De France teaches that France is not simply an academic subject and that language skills are best improved by usage. De France students gain a measure of independence and learn how to trade respect with people of other cultures.

Contact: J.P. Cosnard, Director
333 Christian Street, POB 788
Wallingford, CT 06492

Telephone: 203/269-8355
Fax: 203/269-4555

For-profit corporation (1957)

Destinations: France

40 students outbound from the United States

P R O G R A M   D E S C R I P T I O N S

De France Summer School in Paris
Forty U.S. students study French art history, performing arts, and government. The students are grouped according to their fluency in French. They attend classes six days a week and live with French families in Paris. After four weeks, the students travel with a vacationing French family.

S E L E C T I O N   P R O C E S S

Outbound students complete a formal application process, including interviews and two recommendations.

S U P P O R T   S E R V I C E S

De France staffers accompany students to France and conduct an orientation session in Paris.

DE FRANCE				
Programs	Length of Stay	Ages Served	Approximate Fee	Requirements
De France Summer School in Paris	6 weeks	High school students	$4,800, including transportation and insurance	2 years of high school classes in French

EDUCATIONAL RESOURCE DEVELOPMENT TRUST

With the goal of encouraging intercultural communication as the basic step in achieving world peace and global friendships, ERDT focuses on youth homestays with language training and academic coursework.

Contact: Roger A. Riske, President
475 Washington Blvd., Suite 220
Marina del Rey, CA 90292

Telephone: 310/821-9977
Fax: 310/821-9282

Non-profit corporation (1974)

Destinations: Argentina, Belgium, Brazil, Croatia, Czech Republic, Denmark, France, Georgia, Germany, Italy, Japan, Mexico, Norway, Slovakia, Spain, Sweden, Switzerland, Thailand

6 students outbound from the United States
626 students inbound to the United States

PROGRAM DESCRIPTIONS

Academic Year/Semester Abroad
U.S. students live with screened host families and attend high school. Students may opt for intensive language training as needed.

One-Month Homestay/Farmstay/Ranchstay
International students live with screened U.S. host families on a farm or ranch or in the city. They participate in the host family's daily activities, but they do not attend classes.

Short-Term Group Study Tour
International students travel to the United States to live with host families, take classes in American culture and the English language, and tour historic and recreational sites.

SHARE! High School Exchange Program
International students live with screened U.S. host families and attend high school.

EDUCATIONAL RESOURCE DEVELOPMENT TRUST				
Programs	Length of Stay	Ages Served	Approximate Fee	Requirements
Academic Year/Semester Abroad	1 semester or academic year	16 to 18	Varies greatly, according to the host country and optional language classes	None
1-Month Homestay/ Farmstay/ Ranchstay	4 weeks	15 to 25	$650 to $900, excluding transportation; no fee for host families	None
Short-Term Group Study Tour	2 to 4 weeks	12 to 26	$550 to $1,250, excluding transportation; no fee for host families	None

S E L E C T I O N   P R O C E S S

Outbound students must complete an application form and demonstrate proficiency in the host language and above-average academic performance to qualify for an ERDT exchange. An area representative will interview prospective students.

S U P P O R T   S E R V I C E S

ERDT area representatives provide pre-departure and post-arrival orientation sessions for participating students. They offer counseling support and periodically monitor students' progress.

FOREIGN STUDY LEAGUE

FSL believes that it is through individual experiences that understandings between peoples are established. Our students are provided the opportunity and challenge of becoming part of another family and another culture. The development of language proficiency and lifelong friendships are among the benefits of this program.

Contact: Sarah Reese, Director
1903 Old Swede Road, POB 400
Douglassville, PA 19518

Telephone: 800/USA-4FSL
215/689-4401
Fax: 215/689-4477

For-profit corporation (1989)

Destinations: Austria, Germany, Ireland, Mexico, Russia, Spain

2 students outbound from the United States
238 students inbound to the United States

PROGRAM DESCRIPTIONS

FSL Outbound
U.S. students live with host families in France, Germany, Ireland, Mexico, or Spain. The five- and 10-month programs include enrollment in the local high school; however, students may elect to attend a private school for an additional fee.

FSL Summer Program
International students live with screened U.S. host families while taking intensive courses in English. The program features morning classes and planned day trips to area attractions.

FSL School Year in America
International students live with screened U.S. host families while attending classes at the local high school.

SELECTION PROCESS

Outbound students must complete an application form (including school transcripts, medical forms, and faculty recommendations) by May 1 for September programs and by October 1 for January programs. They must have at least a C+ average and demonstrate positive motivation for going on exchange; also, for its academic programs, FSL may require basic proficiency in the host language. FSL regional coordinators will interview each student.

Scholarships and other financial aid funds are available for qualified students, based on merit, need, and availability of funds.

FOREIGN STUDY LEAGUE				
Programs	Length of Stay	Ages Served	Approximate Fee	Requirements
FSL Outbound	1, 2, 5, or 10 months	High school students	$1,800 for one month to $6,000 for 10 months, including transportation	None
FSL Summer Program	1 month	High school students	$800, excluding transportation; no fee for host families	None
FSL School Year in America	5 or 10 months	High school students	$2,300 (five months) to $3,100 (10 months), excluding transportation; no fee for host families	None

Host families of inbound students must submit an application and references. FSL regional coordinators will interview each family in the home.

SUPPORT SERVICES

FSL provides pre-departure and post-arrival orientation sessions for students, as well as handbooks for further study. Trained FSL coordinators monitor students' progress, filing written progress reports every other month.

THE FOUNDATION FOR INTERNATIONAL UNDERSTANDING

Dedicated to peace through understanding, the Foundation for International Understanding emphasizes a strong language/ cultural education component with the homestay aspect of youth exchange.

Contact: Jeanne Steinleitner, Director
6225 Lusk Blvd.
San Diego, CA 92121

Telephone: 619/455-1122
Fax: 619/535-1777

Non-profit corporation (1988)

Destinations: Brazil, France, Japan, Spain

21 students outbound from the United States
1,364 students inbound to the United States

PROGRAM DESCRIPTIONS

Summer in Japan
U.S. students live with screened Japanese host families while they study Japanese culture and visit historic sites in the Tokyo area.

Short Homestay in America
International students live with screened U.S. host families, study American culture and the English language, and take part in special cultural activities.

THE FOUNDATION FOR INTERNATIONAL UNDERSTANDING				
Programs	Length of Stay	Ages Served	Approximate Fee	Requirements
Summer in Japan	2 weeks	13 to 21	$1,700, including transportation	None
Short Homestay in America	2 to 4 weeks	13 to 25	$200 per week, excluding transportation; no fee for host families	None
High School Experience	2 to 4 weeks	14 to 18	$225 per week, excluding transportation; no fee for host families	None
Intensive English Program	2 to 4 weeks	15 to 18	$140 per week, excluding transportation	None

High School Experience

International students live with screened U.S. host families and take classes in the local high school (as well as additional English courses). These students "shadow" American students through their daily routines.

Intensive English Program

International students take part in an academic program to prepare students to join an American high school year program. They will study the English language, U.S. history and government, and American family life.

SELECTION PROCESS

Outbound students complete an application form and undergo a screening by a network of FIU "teacher/guides" and field managers.

Host families of inbound students undergo the same process.

SUPPORT SERVICES

FIU conducts orientation sessions for its students and offers counseling support. Also, FIU programs include an educational component— three-hour classes held four times weekly—to guide students through the cultural changes they will experience during the exchange.

FULBRIGHT-GESELLSCHAFT

Organized in 1967 by alumni of the Fulbright scholarship program, Fulbright-Gesellschaft furthers scientific, cultural, and educational youth exchanges as direct swaps between individual American and German students.

Contact: Admissions
12801 Saddlebrook Drive
Silver Spring, MD 20906

Telephone: 800/258-5592
Fax: 301/946-8708

Non-profit corporation (1986)

Destinations: Germany

Numbers of students not available

PROGRAM   DESCRIPTIONS

Three-Week Exchange
U.S. and German students live with host families and attend a host secondary school. A teacher serves as the Fulbright coordinator accompanying groups of 15 or more students. The program—in June for U.S. students to Germany, and in April for German students to the United States—includes two or three local sightseeing trips, as well as orientation sessions prior to departure and during the exchange.

Term Exchange
U.S. and German students live with host families and attend a host secondary school. The trip includes comprehensive orientation and counseling support.

FULBRIGHT-GESELLSCHAFT				
Programs	Length of Stay	Ages Served	Approximate Fee	Requirements
3-Week Exchange	3 weeks	14 to 18	$350, excluding transportation; no fee for host families	None
Term Exchange	3 to 5 months	15 to 18	$750 to $1,450, excluding transportation; no fee for host families	Language proficiency required
Year Exchange	10 months	15 to 18	$2,400, excluding transportation; no fee for host families	Language proficiency required

Year Exchange
U.S. and German students live with host families and attend a host secondary school. Pre-departure and post-arrival orientation sessions will be conducted.

SELECTION PROCESS
Contact Fulbright-Gesellschaft directly for application information.

SUPPORT SERVICES
Besides the extensive orientation and counseling opportunities available, the Fulbright coordinators develop additional out-of-classroom programs for students during the exchange.

IBEROAMERICAN CULTURAL EXCHANGE PROGRAM

ICEP serves to promote the study of Spanish in the United States and the study of English abroad through homestay programs for high school students.

Contact: Bonnie P. Mortell, Executive Director
13920 93rd Avenue, NE
Kirkland, WA 98034

Telephone: 206/821-1463
Fax: 206/821-1849

Non-profit corporation (1970)

Destinations: Bolivia, Costa Rica, Guatemala, Mexico, Peru, Spain

95 students outbound to the United States
112 students inbound to the United States

PROGRAM DESCRIPTIONS

Outbound Mexico Homestay Program
U.S. students live with screened host families and attend high school in Mexico (when in session).

IBEROAMERICAN CULTURAL EXCHANGE PROGRAM

Programs	Length of Stay	Ages Served	Approximate Fee	Requirements
Outbound Mexico Homestay Program	6 weeks to 1 academic year	15 to 18	$725 to $2,100, excluding transportation and insurance	None
Outbound Costa Rica, Guatemala, and Bolivia Homestay Program	6 weeks to 1 semester	15 to 18	$725 to $2,100, excluding transportation and insurance	None
Exchange Visitor Program	3 months to 1 academic year	15 to 18	$1,800 to $2,500, excluding transportation and insurance; no fee for host families	None

Outbound Costa Rica, Guatemala, and Bolivia Homestay Program

U.S. students live with screened host families in Costa Rica, Guatemala, or Bolivia. They attend high school in the host country (when in session).

Exchange Visitor Program

International students from Spanish-speaking countries live with screened U.S. host families, attend high school, and serve as a Spanish language aide for part of each school day.

SELECTION PROCESS

Outbound students and *host families of inbound students* undergo careful screening by ICEP national offices and local coordinators.

SUPPORT SERVICES

Pre-departure and re-entry orientation sessions will be conducted by local representatives in Mexico City, Miami, or the home country; also, counseling will be provided by local representatives in the host city. ICEP provides supplemental teaching materials to U.S. teachers of Spanish.

INTERCAMBIO INTERNACIONAL DE ESTUDIANTES, A.C.

Intercambio sponsors the interchange of students so that young people will become a part of a home abroad. Students participate in all activities of the host family, so that they may know as fully as possible the cultural and social structures of the country they visit, as a basis for lasting peace.

Contact: Laura Hatch, Program Manager
16 Broadway, Suite 107
Fargo, ND 58102

Telephone: 800/437-4170
701/232-1776
Fax: 701/232-1670

Non-profit corporation (1991)

Destinations: Canada, Costa Rica, El Salvador, Guatemala, Mexico, Panama

29 students outbound from the United States
437 students inbound to the United States

P R O G R A M   D E S C R I P T I O N S

Summer Outbound Program
U.S. students live with screened host families in Costa Rica, Guatemala, or Mexico in the summer and attend high school (except in Mexico, where students will arrive after the close of the academic year).

Summer Inbound Program
Mexican students live with screened U.S. host families in the summer.

INTERCAMBIO INTERNACIONAL DE ESTUDIANTES, A.C.				
Programs	Length of Stay	Ages Served	Approximate Fee	Requirements
Summer Outbound Program	8 weeks	12 to 16	$1,300 to $1,650, including transportation and insurance	None
Summer Inbound Program	8 to 9 weeks	11 to 16	$1,500 to $1,800, including transportation and insurance; no fee for host families	None
Winter Inbound Program	8 to 9 weeks	11 to 16	$1,500 to $1,800, including transportation and insurance; no fee for host families	None

Winter Inbound Program

Students from Central American countries live with screened U.S. host families in the winter. They take classes in local school on an audit basis.

SELECTION PROCESS

Outbound students must complete an application form and take part in a formal interview. Medical and academic records must be included in the application, along with a letter from the student expressing his or her reasons for going on exchange. Students coming to the United States must know some English. The deadline is March 30 for the Summer Outbound Program, March 15 for the Summer Inbound Program, and September 15 for the Winter Inbound Program.

Host families of inbound students must complete an application form, with references from sources such as church leaders and school officials. Local Intercambio representatives then interview the family.

SUPPORT SERVICES

Intercambio provides pre-departure orientation sessions for students. Trained volunteers offer counseling in the host country as needed. Host families receive a handbook and "culturgrams" to prepare for their students. Chaperones travel with the students to and from the host country.

INTERNATIONAL CHRISTIAN YOUTH EXCHANGE

The International Christian Youth Exchange offers homestay exchanges, workcamp projects, and issues conferences to young people from selected countries, without reference to religious affiliation.

Contact: Andrea Spencer-Linzie, Executive Director
134 West 26th Street
New York, NY 10001

Telephone: 212/206-7307
Fax: 212/633-9085

Non-profit corporation (1948)

Destinations: Australia, Austria, Belgium, Bolivia, Brazil, Colombia, Costa Rica, Denmark, Finland, France, Germany, Ghana, Honduras, Iceland, India, Italy, Japan, Korea, Mexico, New Zealand, Nigeria, Norway, Poland, Sierra Leone, Sweden, Switzerland, Taiwan

80 students outbound from the United States
80 students inbound to the United States

PROGRAM DESCRIPTIONS

Year-Long Outbound Program

Students from ICYE countries ages 16 to 18 attend school, live with screened host families, and may also do volunteer service projects. Exchangees ages 19 to 30 volunteer full-time with a social service agency, living with a host family or at the site of the volunteer work. The program also includes language training and "issues conferences," exposing students to current affairs from the perspective of their host country.

International Workcamps

Students from ICYE countries travel in groups of 10 to 25 to Africa, Europe, Latin America, and the United States to perform "workcamp projects"—usually some form of rural development or environmental reclamation activity.

Host Program

International students live with screened U.S. host families. In some cases, depending upon the student's age, he or she will live in the dormitory facilities of a community service agency. Students take part in high school classes and volunteer community projects. The program

INTERNATIONAL CHRISTIAN YOUTH EXCHANGE				
Programs	Length of Stay	Ages Served	Approximate Fee	Requirements
Year-Long Outbound Program	1 year	16 to 30	$4,950, including transportation, insurance, and a small amount of spending money; no fee for host families	None
International Workcamps	2 to 4 weeks	16 and older	$250 to $2,600, including transportation, insurance, and selected leisure activities.	None
Host Program	1 year	16 to 24	Host families agree to provide room, board, and a small monthly stipend to students; ICYE cover other expenses.	None

includes language training, issues conferences, and planned recreational activities.

SELECTION PROCESS

Outbound students must complete an application form available from the ICYE office in New York. Applicants will be evaluated by ICYE without regard to their religious backgrounds.

Host families of inbound students must complete an application and provide appropriate references to the ICYE office in New York.

SUPPORT SERVICES

ICYE issues handbooks to participants as they begin pre-departure orientation sessions. Throughout the year, regional volunteers maintain contact with all participants. Students, host families, and school personnel attend conferences. Short-term language training is given to students after they arrive in the host country. ICYE conducts issues conferences and solicits evaluations from students and host families throughout the exchange.

INTERNATIONAL EDUCATION FORUM

IEF provides international and American students with the opportunity to increase their global understanding through homestay experiences— the practical exercise of living together and knowing other cultures. We offer individuals and groups the opportunity to live and learn in more than 31 countries, from one week to a full academic year.

Contact:　Wayne F. Brewer, President/CEO
Box 460M, 1590 Union Blvd.
Bay Shore, NY 11706

Telephone:　516/968-0554
Fax:　　　　516/968-0553

Non-profit corporation (1981)

Destinations:　Australia, Austria, Belgium, Brazil, Canada, Colombia, Commonwealth of Independent States, Costa Rica, Croatia, Czech Republic, Denmark, Egypt, Finland, France, Germany, Hong Kong, Hungary, Italy, Japan,

Mexico, Netherlands, Norway, Poland, Portugal, Reunion, Romania, Spain, Sweden, Thailand, Yugoslavia

453 students outbound from the United States
7,731 students inbound to the United States

PROGRAM DESCRIPTIONS

Group Spring or Summer Programs Overseas
U.S. students take part in a group homestay/travel program—living with a screened host family for the entire stay, staying in hotels, or combining the two. Planned excursions and sightseeing trips are included.

Overseas Academic Year Programs
U.S. students live with screened host families in Australia, France, Germany, or Spain and attend high school.

Group School Year Programs
International students travel in groups to visit a host school or English-as-a-Second-Language (ESL) program. The program includes homestays, planned excursions, and group recreational activities.

Group Summer Programs
International students take part in a group homestay/study program. Each trip may include ESL classes, planned excursions, and group recreational activities.

INTERNATIONAL EDUCATION FORUM				
Programs	Length of Stay	Ages Served	Approximate Fee	Requirements
Group Spring or Summer Programs Overseas	1 to 4 weeks	13 to 21	$995 to $2,500, including transportation and insurance	None
Overseas Academic Year Programs	5 to 12 months	14 to 18	$4,500 to $5,500, including international transportation and insurance	None
Group School Year Programs	1 to 3 weeks	13 to 19	$500 to $700, excluding transportation and insurance; no fee for host families	None
Group Summer Programs	1 to 8 weeks	13 to 21	$500 to $900, excluding transportation and insurance; no fee for host families	None
Academic Year Programs	3 to 12 months	15 to 17	$1,500 to $4,000, excluding transportation; no fee for host families	A strong command of English

Academic Year Programs

International students live with screened U.S. host families and attend high school.

SELECTION PROCESS

Outbound students must complete an application form and host family letter. Academic Year Program students must also submit academic and medical histories and letters from their parents. Students will be interviewed by IEF representatives. Deadlines vary with each program.

Host families of inbound students must complete an application form; also, they are interviewed by an IEF representative. They will be chosen no later than three weeks prior to the students' arrival date.

SUPPORT SERVICES

IEF conducts orientation sessions for departing and arriving students, as well as for host families. Local representatives provide counseling support as needed. Students and families receive handbooks to consult during the trip. Extensive evaluations are solicited from students and families during the trip. For group programs, chaperones and/or teachers accompany the group.

INTERNATIONAL STUDENT EXCHANGE

The purpose of International Student Exchange is to promote worldwide peace and understanding, to develop intercultural friendships and family relationships, to provide a sound educational program for participants, and to facilitate sharing among families, schools, communities, and students.

Contact: Frank Broomfield, Vice President
11219 N. Highway 3, POB 840
Fort Jones, CA 96032

Telephone: 800/766-4656
916/468-2264
Fax: 916/468-2060

Non-profit corporation (1982)

INTERNATIONAL STUDENT EXCHANGE				
Programs	Length of Stay	Ages Served	Approximate Fee	Requirements
School Year Abroad Program	1 academic year	16 to 18	$2,800 to $7,700 (depending on the host country), excluding transportation	None
3-Month Summer Program	3 months	15 to 18	$1,800, excluding transportation; no fee for host families	None
6-Month Study Program	6 months	15 to 18	$2,700, excluding transportation; no fee for host families	None
10-Month School Year Program	10 months	15 to 18	$2,800, excluding transportation; no fee for host families	
1-Year Study Program	1 year	At least 15	$3,800, excluding transportation; no fee for host families	None

Destinations: Bolivia, Brazil, Colombia, Croatia, Egypt, France, Germany, Hungary, Italy, Japan, Luxembourg, Mexico, Norway, People's Republic of China, Spain, Thailand, Turkey

10 students outbound from the United States
450 students inbound to the United States

PROGRAM DESCRIPTIONS

School Year Abroad Program
U.S. students live with screened host families in France, Germany, Italy, Japan, Mexico, or Spain.

Three-Month Summer Program
International students live with screened U.S. host families during the summer. Family life and cultural awareness are focal points of the stay.

Six-Month Study Program
International students live with screened U.S. host families for the spring or fall academic semester. They attend classes at the local high school.

Ten-Month School Year Program
International students live with screened U.S. host families and attend classes at the local high school.

One-Year Study Program
International students live with screened U.S. host families and attend classes at the local high school.

SELECTION PROCESS

Outbound students apply through ISE's national office. Each student completes an application which includes an information sheet, autobiographical statement, school transcripts, health questionnaire, medical treatment authorization form, language evaluation, contract, and personal references. Also, students will be interviewed by a national representative. Deadlines range from 60 to 90 days before the program date.

Host families of inbound students complete an application form, including personal references. ISE representatives interview the family in the home. Applications are accepted throughout the year.

SUPPORT SERVICES

Students receive a handbook during ISE pre-departure orientation session. After students arrive in the host country, ISE conducts a post-arrival orientation session with the host families. Trained counselors are on call in the host country to provide assistance as needed.

INTERNATIONAL TRAVEL STUDY

Originally begun to foster short cultural homestays for U.S. students, ITS now sponsors a wide range of exchange programs, including a special focus on groups chaperoned by accompanying teachers.

Contact: James Hyland, Jr., President
5700 Fourth Street North
St. Petersburg, FL 33703

Telephone: 813/525-9696
Fax: 813/525-1383

For-profit corporation (1977)

Destinations: Australia, Brazil, Bulgaria, Canada, Commonwealth of Independent States, Czech Republic, France, Germany, Greece, Hungary, Ireland, Italy, Monaco, Netherlands, Spain, Switzerland, United Kingdom, Vatican City, Yugoslavia

460 students outbound from the United States
405 students inbound to the United States

PROGRAM DESCRIPTIONS

Cultural Experience with a Host Family Abroad
U.S. students live with French host families, including a sponsored host family activity each week. In some cases, students travel as part of a larger group, composed of compatible students from different regions of the United States.

Comparative Cultures Study Tour
Groups of 42 U.S. students—traveling with seven teachers and an administrator—tour major capital cities in Europe. Working with ITS, groups may tailor their itineraries to meet specific educational goals.

Cultural Experience with a Host Family in the United States
International students travel (as individuals or in compatible groups) to sites in the United States. When possible, students live with U.S. host families and visit schools. Weekly host family activities will also be provided where appropriate.

Academic Semester/Year with a Host Family in the United States
International students live with screened U.S. host families and attend local high schools.

INTERNATIONAL TRAVEL STUDY				
Programs	Length of Stay	Ages Served	Approximate Fee	Requirements
Cultural Experience with a Host Family Abroad	3 to 4 weeks	15 to 18	$400 to $450, excluding transportation and insurance	A working knowledge of French
Comparative Cultures Study Tour	14 to 28 days	15 to 18	$1,500 to $2,800, including transportation and insurance	None
Cultural Experience with a Host Family in the United States	3 to 4 weeks	14 to 18	$290 to $500, excluding transportation; no fee for host families	None
Academic Semester/ Year with a Host Family in the United States	1 semester or academic year	15 to 17	$1,650 (semester) to $2,150 (year), excluding transportation and insurance; no fee for host families	A working knowledge of English

SELECTION PROCESS

Outbound students must complete an application form and submit written recommendations from school officials.

Host families of inbound students must complete an application and be interviewed by ITS staffers.

SUPPORT SERVICES

ITS conducts orientations for students before departure. Also, staffers monitor students' progress throughout the stay and arrange weekly activities (for certain programs). ITS groups will be served by Resident Assistant Personnel who serve as counselors during various stops in the host country.

INTRAX—INTERNATIONAL TRAINING AND EXCHANGE

The goal of INTRAX is to provide international students with an opportunity to share daily life with an American or Canadian host family and participate in academics and cultural activities. INTRAX offers an Academic Program which includes 12 hours of classes per week, a Cultural Program which excludes the academic portion, and the Individual Program with neither academics or planned activities.

Contact: Anna Lamassonne, Program Manager
One Post Street, Suite 700
San Francisco, CA 94104

Telephone: 800/288-1221
415/434-1221
Fax: 415/986-4620

For-profit corporation (1983)

Destinations: Austria, Czech Republic, Denmark, France, Germany, Hungary, Italy, Japan, Macedonia, Mexico, Poland, Slovakia, Slovenia, Spain, Switzerland, Taiwan

16 students outbound from the United States
4,600 students inbound to the United States

INTRAX—INTERNATIONAL TRAINING AND EXCHANGE				
Programs	Length of Stay	Ages Served	Approximate Fee	Requirements
Academic Homestay Program	2 to 4 weeks	15 to 21	$2,000 to $2,500, excluding transportation; no fee for host families	None
Cultural Homestay Program	2 to 4 weeks	15 to 21	$1,500 to $2,000, excluding transportation; no fee for host families	None
Individual Homestay Program	2 to 6 weeks	16 to 22	$1,000 to $1,200, excluding transportation; no fee for host families	A working knowledge of English
Intensive English Program	8 weeks for each proficiency level	High school students	$1,950 for each eight-week session, excluding transportation	None

PROGRAM DESCRIPTIONS

Academic Homestay Program
International students live with screened U.S. host families, attend English language classes, and participate in planned excursions and community activities. INTRAX coordinates similar outbound programs for U.S. students on an individual basis, as requested.

Cultural Homestay Program
International students experience a cross-cultural exchange with U.S. host families. While there are no formal classes, students will take part in planned recreational and cultural activities with their host families.

Individual Homestay Program
International students live with screened U.S. host families.

Intensive English Program
The INTRAX English Institute at Widener University in Chester, Pa., provides year-round intensive English as a Second Language courses at six proficiency levels, from beginning to advanced. Small classes of 15 students receive 25 hours of classroom instruction per week, complemented by an interactive computer language laboratory. The institute also provides a variety of student support services and extracurricular activities.

SELECTION PROCESS

Outbound students must file an application form, faculty recommendation, and medical release to qualify for INTRAX programs. Personal interviews are not required. The deadline for applications is three weeks prior to the date of arrival in the host country.

Host families of inbound students complete an application form; then, INTRAX program coordinators interview each family in the home.

SUPPORT SERVICES

INTRAX offers orientations for host families and students, who also receive exchange manuals for later reference. Trained local volunteers are available as needed for counseling.

THE IRISH AMERICAN CULTURAL INSTITUTE

The Irish Way program offers an immersion in Irish life and culture through classroom study, field trips, a homestay, and other educational experiences. Students will attain an understanding of important figures in Irish history and literature and a beginning knowledge of both the Irish language and Irish-American history.

Contact: John Walsh, Chairman
3 Elm St., Suite 204
Morristown, NJ 07960

Telephone: 201/605-1991

Non-profit corporation (1976)

Destinations: Ireland

100 students outbound from the United States

PROGRAM DESCRIPTIONS

The Irish Way
U.S. students are immersed in Irish life and culture through classroom study, field trips, a homestay experience, and other educational experiences.

THE IRISH AMERICAN CULTURAL INSTITUTE				
Programs	Length of Stay	Ages Served	Approximate Fee	Requirements
The Irish Way	5 weeks	Students who have completed 9th grade	$2,150, excluding transportation	None

SELECTION PROCESS

Outbound students complete a questionnaire which includes a brief essay question on why they wish to participate in The Irish Way. Transcripts and recommendations from advisors are requested. Parents are also asked to write their reasons for wanting their children to participate.

About half of the students participating in The Irish Way receive financial assistance, usually in the range of $1,000 (though some larger scholarships are awarded). Scholarship criteria are financial need and evidence of previous interest in Irish culture. Scholarship applications are sent only on request.

SUPPORT SERVICES

Students receive a handbook. In larger communities, pre-departure orientation meetings are held.

LEGACY INTERNATIONAL

Legacy International offers students around the world an opportunity to build bridges of understanding between people of diverse cultures. Legacy's programs are based on the belief that, when provided the time, place, and circumstances, young people can gain practical tools to create a promising future for our rapidly changing world.

Contact: Mary Helmig, Co-Director
Route 4, POB 265
Bedford, VA 24523

Telephone: 703/297-5982
Fax: 703/297-1860

Non-profit corporation (1979)

Destinations: Brazil, Canada, Colombia, Commonwealth of Independent States, Costa Rica, Czech Republic, Djibouti, France, Ghana, Hungary, Ireland, Israel, Japan, Kenya, Korea, Mexico, Morocco, Nigeria, Puerto Rico, Senegal, Spain, Turkey, Venezuela

20 students outbound from the United States
80 students inbound to the United States

LEGACY INTERNATIONAL				
Programs	Length of Stay	Ages Served	Approximate Fee	Requirements
Summer Training Program	3 to 6 weeks	15 to 18	$1,400 to $2,500 per 3-week session, excluding transportation	None
Youth Program	4 to 8 weeks	11 to 14	$2,000 to $3,000, excluding transportation	None
Native American Sojourn	4 weeks	15 to 18	$2,250, excluding transportation	None
Costa Rica and France Adventure Programs	4 weeks	15 to 18	Contact Legacy directly for fees	At least 2 years of high school classes in French or Spanish

PROGRAM DESCRIPTIONS

Summer Training Program

U.S. and international students live together in a "global community" in Bedford, Va. Living in wood-frame cabins with 10 to 14 other students, participants take part in non-academic workshops focused on global issues and communication skills. Other program activities include special guest speakers, field trips, cultural festivals, and performances. International students will take part in sightseeing excursions and optional homestays.

Youth Program

U.S. and international students live together in a residential program in Bedford, Va. The program includes morning and afternoon classes, as well as recreational activities to teach character development and cross-cultural communication. Weekend homestays and regional sightseeing excursions are optional.

Native American Sojourn

U.S. and international students travel to North Carolina to experience life among Native Americans. Students live in camps and hostels, with optional homestays. Weekend excursions include state parks, beaches, and historic sites. Another aspect of the program is service projects in Native American areas.

Costa Rica and France Adventure Programs

U.S. students live with screened host families, participating in recreational activities and internships as well as weekend excursions.

SELECTION PROCESS

Outbound students must file an application form and two letters of recommendation from teachers and friends. Also, they must complete an interview with a Legacy representative. The deadline for Legacy programs is May 30.

Host families of inbound families complete application forms and a personal interview. No recommendations are required.

SUPPORT SERVICES

Legacy provides orientation sessions for students and host families, as well as counseling support from trained staffers as needed.

NACEL CULTURAL EXCHANGES

Since its beginning, more than 95,000 students and families have participated in NACEL exchanges. These programs are administered by language teachers who want to promote international understanding through organized, affordable homestays.

Contact: Admissions
3410 Federal Drive, Suite 101
St. Paul, MN 55122

Telephone: 612/686-0080
Fax: 612/686-9601

Non-profit corporation (1969)

Destinations: Commonwealth of Independent States, France, Germany, Ireland, Ivory Coast, Mexico, Spain

Numbers of students not available

PROGRAM DESCRIPTIONS

Summer Homestays Abroad
U.S. students live with host families in France, Germany, the Ivory Coast, Mexico, or Spain during the summer.

Summer Homestays Abroad (Ireland or Russia)

U.S. students travel to Ireland or Russia during the summer. Living with host families, they will take morning classes and field trips (academic credit depends upon home school policies).

Summer Language Camps Abroad

U.S. students live at a school in Paris, France, taking three weeks of language classes following NACEL's curriculum. The program includes cultural experiences designed to augment the formal language training. One native teacher and one American teacher work with 10 students, to maximize results.

Semester Abroad/School Year Abroad

U.S. students live with host families in France or Spain for the fall semester or an academic year.

Summer Hosting Program

French, German, or Spanish students live with host families in the United States during the summer.

School Year Hosting in the United States

French and Spanish students live with U.S. host families for an academic year. They attend classes in the local high school.

NACEL CULTURAL EXCHANGES				
Programs	Length of Stay	Ages Served	Approximate Fee	Requirements
Summer Homestays Abroad	3 to 4 weeks	13 to 18	$1,295 to $2,145, including transportation	None
Summer Homestays Abroad (Ireland or Russia)	3 weeks	13 to 18	$1,835 to $2,345, including transportation	None
Summer Language Camps Abroad	3 weeks	13 to 16	$2,295 to $2,645, including transportation	None
Semester Abroad/School Year Abroad	1 semester or academic year	16 to 19	$2,895 (including transportation) for the semester, or $3,995 (including transportation) for the year	None
Summer Hosting Program	1 month	13 to 18	$1,295 to $1,595, including transportation; no fee for host families	None
School Year Hosting in the United States	1 academic year	15 to 18	$4,145, including transportation; no fee for host families	None

SELECTION PROCESS

Outbound students submit applications and references to NACEL's area coordinators, who conduct a personal interview with each student. Many summer, semester, and year programs require two years of instruction in the host language and above-average grades to qualify.

Host families of inbound students must complete an application form, submit references, and be interviewed by a NACEL area coordinator.

SUPPORT SERVICES

Pre-departure and post-arrival orientation sessions are conducted for most programs. NACEL chaperones conduct groups of students to the host country, and NACEL area coordinators provide local counseling as needed.

NATIONAL ASSOCIATION OF SECONDARY SCHOOL PRINCIPALS, SCHOOL PARTNERSHIPS, INTERNATIONAL

School Partnerships, International began in 1972 as a department of NASSP—a professional association of more than 43,000 school administrators—to organize short-term, school-to-school pairings and to foster cultural and academic exchanges among the participating schools.

Contact: Marisa Sherard, Director
1904 Association Drive
Reston, VA 22091

Telephone: 703/860-0200
Fax: 703/476-5432

Non-profit corporation (1916)

Destinations: Austria, Canada, Commonwealth of Independent States, Costa Rica, France, Germany, Italy, Japan, Mexico, Spain, United Kingdom

NATIONAL ASSOCIATION OF SECONDARY SCHOOL PRINCIPALS, SCHOOL PARTNERSHIPS, INTERNATIONAL				
Programs	Length of Stay	Ages Served	Approximate Fee	Requirements
School Partnerships, International Program	3 to 4 weeks	High school students	$700 to $1,990, including transportation	None

2,039 students outbound from the United States
1,730 students inbound to the United States

PROGRAM DESCRIPTIONS

School Partnerships, International Program

U.S. secondary schools will be paired with a counterpart school abroad. Beginning with informational exchanges, the schools ultimately will trade groups of five to 15 students and a faculty member. Students live with host families, attend classes, and take part in school activities. NASSP also coordinates a "Partners of North America Program" for similar exchanges between U.S. and Canadian high schools.

SELECTION PROCESS

Specific requirements for *outbound students* and *host families of inbound students* will be governed by the goals of each exchange agreement; however, no specific language ability is required in most cases.

Orientation sessions are conducted prior to departure from the United States. Additional orientations are offered in the host countries by co-sponsors.

SUPPORT SERVICES

Orientation sessions are conducted prior to departure from the United States. Additional orientations are offered in the host countries by co-sponsors.

NATIONAL FFA ORGANIZATION

The FFA—a national association comprised of students preparing for careers in agriculture—operates its exchange programs to provide young people the opportunity to experience a new culture while studying international agriculture.

Also known as Future Farmers of America.

Contact: Diane Crow, Student Services Specialist/International
5632 Mt. Vernon Memorial Highway
POB 15160
Alexandria, VA 22309

Telephone: 703/360-3600
Fax: 703/360-5524

Non-profit corporation (1928)

Destinations: Australia, Bulgaria, Costa Rica, Germany, Greece, Japan, Thailand

> 5 students outbound from the United States
> 93 students inbound to the United States

PROGRAM DESCRIPTIONS

World AgriSciences Studies Program

U.S. and international students live with screened host families involved in agriculture. They study agriculture and a general curriculum in the local high school.

Japan Short Program

U.S. and Japanese students live with screened host families as they study relationships between the agricultural systems of both countries.

SELECTION PROCESS

Outbound students must have an interest in agriculture to qualify for the programs. They complete an application form, including school transcripts and recommendations, and take part in an interview.

Host families of inbound students also submit application forms and take part in an interview. They must be involved in agriculture to qualify.

SUPPORT SERVICES

The National FFA Organization provides orientation sessions and counseling support to participating students.

NATIONAL FFA ORGANIZATION				
Programs	Length of Stay	Ages Served	Approximate Fee	Requirements
World AgriSciences Studies Program	1 semester or academic year	15 to 19	$3,100 for U.S. students, including transportation; no fee for host families	None
Japan Short Program	3 to 4 weeks	16 to 19	$2,400, including transportation; no fee for host families	None

OPEN DOOR STUDENT EXCHANGE

Open Door Student Exchange provides homestay and study opportunities for U.S. and international students.

Contact: Frank Tarsitano, Executive Vice President
839 Stewart Avenue
Garden City, NY 11530
Telephone: 516/745-6232
Non-profit corporation (1964)

Destinations: Argentina, Australia, Bolivia, Brazil, Bulgaria, Canada, Chile, Colombia, Commonwealth of Independent States, Costa Rica, Czech Republic, Denmark, Ecuador, Egypt, France, Germany, Hungary, Indonesia, Israel, Italy, Japan, Latvia, Lithuania, Mexico, Paraguay, Poland, Romania, Russia, Slovakia, Spain, Sweden, Thailand, Uruguay

100 students outbound from the United States
600 students inbound to the United States

PROGRAM DESCRIPTIONS

Summer/Semester/School Year Abroad
U.S. students live with screened host families and attend classes in the local high school (when in session). The semester and year programs offer an optional tour of the host country.

Congress Bundestag
U.S. students who are graduating seniors from high school vocational programs in selected states may be eligible under this program for full scholarships to undertake work/study programs in Germany.

School Visit/Semester/School Year Program in the United States
International students live with screened U.S. host families and attend classes in the local high school (on an audit basis, in the School Visit Program).

SELECTION PROCESS

Outbound students and *host families of inbound students* must complete an application and take part in an interview with Open Door representatives. Scholarship assistance is available to qualified stu-

OPEN DOOR STUDENT EXCHANGE				
Programs	Length of Stay	Ages Served	Approximate Fee	Requirements
Summer/ Semester/School Year Abroad	4 to 8 weeks (summer), 5 months (semester), or 10 months (year)	15 to 18	$2,300 to $3,500 (summer), $3,200 to $4,500 (semester), or $4,200 to $4,500 (year), including transportation	None
Congress Bundestag	1 year	Graduating high school seniors	$0 (full scholarship)	Contact Open Door for more details
School Visit/ Semester/School Year Program in the United States	3, 5, or 10 months	15 to 18	$2,150 to $2,600 (school visit), $2,200 to $3,050 (semester), or $2,500 to $3,500 (year), excluding transportation; no fee for host families	A working knowledge of English

dents, including U.S. students who have served earlier as hosts for Open Door international students.

SUPPORT SERVICES

Open Door area representatives provide pre- departure and post-arrival orientation sessions for students.

PACE INSTITUTE INTERNATIONAL

PACE is an international educational foundation offering educational and cultural exchange programs for high school students. PACE's primary concern is insuring that students and families adjust to the dynamics of the exchange and gain full benefits from the program.

Contact: Rick Anaya, President
POB 315
Brightwaters, NY 11718

Telephone: 800/422-PACE

Non-profit corporation (1988)

PACE INSTITUTE INTERNATIONAL				
Programs	Length of Stay	Ages Served	Approximate Fee	Requirements
Academic Year Abroad	1 semester or academic year	15 to 18	Contact PACE directly for fees	At least 2 years of formal training in the host language
Short-Term Programs	2 to 8 weeks	13 to 25	Contact PACE directly for fees	None
Immersion Program	Several weeks or months	16 to 25	Contact PACE directly for fees	None
Scholarship Abroad	4 weeks	15 to 19	$0 (full scholarship); contact PACE for details	None

Destinations: Brazil, Denmark, Finland, France, Germany, Italy, Japan, Mexico, New Zealand, Norway, Romania, Spain, Sweden, Switzerland, Taiwan, Thailand, Yugoslavia

23 students outbound from the United States
1,008 students inbound to the United States

PROGRAM DESCRIPTIONS

Academic Year Abroad

U.S. students live with screened host families and attend the local high school.

International students live with screened U.S. host families and attend the local high school.

Short-Term Programs

International students live with screened U.S. host families as part of a group study tour. They take English language classes, visit historic and cultural sites, and take excursions to popular attractions.

Study tours can be also arranged for groups of U.S. students traveling to Brazil, Japan, Spain, Switzerland, or Thailand.

Immersion Program

U.S. students live with screened host families and take language classes (where available).

International students live with screened U.S. host families and take English classes (where available).

Scholarship Abroad

Five full scholarship trips will be awarded annually to U.S. students for homestays abroad.

SELECTION PROCESS

Outbound students and *host families of inbound students* submit application forms and recommendation letters to PACE. PACE staffers then conduct personal interviews.

The Scholarship Abroad program is open to students who have previously hosted an academic semester/year student. The applicant must submit an essay describing how he or she will benefit from studying abroad, along with three letters of recommendation from faculty members.

SUPPORT SERVICES

PACE staffers provide pre-departure and post-arrival orientation sessions for students.

PEOPLE TO PEOPLE HIGH SCHOOL STUDENT AMBASSADOR PROGRAM

The People to People Student Ambassador Program is designed to help prepare American high school and junior high school students for their roles as responsible citizens and leaders, by offering an opportunity to discover for themselves the economic, political, and cultural factors that influence the world community. The programs are based on the belief that the steps toward peace begin with people, rather than with governments.

Also known as Student Ambassador Program; Friendship Caravan; Initiative for Understanding; Youth Science Exchange.

Contact: Paul M. Watson, Associate Director
Dwight D. Eisenhower Building
110 South Ferrall Street
Spokane, WA 99202

Telephone: 509/534-0430
Fax: 509/534-5245

For-profit corporation (1963)
Parent organization: People to People (non-profit, 1963)

Destinations: Australia, Austria, Commonwealth of Independent States, Costa Rica, Czech Republic, Denmark, Estonia, Finland, France, Germany, Hong Kong, Hungary, Latvia, Lithuania, Netherlands, New Zealand, People's Republic of China, Poland, Spain, Sweden, Switzerland, United Kingdom

5,636 students outbound from the United States
100 students inbound to the United States

PROGRAM DESCRIPTIONS

Student Ambassador Program
U.S. students take part in educational programs traveling through various parts of the world. Students live with screened host families for five days in each country visited. As they arrive in each city, students attend briefings and take field trips to learn firsthand about the country's history and culture.

Initiative for Understanding
U.S. students travel to the Commonwealth of Independent States and the People's Republic of China. Homestay visits will be scheduled with selected families.

People to People Youth Science Exchange
U.S. and Canadian secondary school students with an interest in science travel to Australia, the Commonwealth of Independent States, Costa Rica, New Zealand, or the People's Republic of China. Students

PEOPLE TO PEOPLE HIGH SCHOOL STUDENT AMBASSADOR PROGRAM				
Programs	Length of Stay	Ages Served	Approximate Fee	Requirements
Student Ambassador Program	3 to 4 weeks	Grades 7 through 12	$3,475 to $3,975, including transportation	None
Initiative for Understanding	23 days	Grades 7 through 12	$3,475 to $3,675, including transportation	None
People to People Youth Science Exchange	3 weeks	High school students	$3,485 to $3,975, including transportation	None
Friendship Caravan	21 days	Grades 7 through 12	$3,650 to $3,885, including transportation	None

visit science camps with advanced programs in aerospace, archaeology, marine biology, or physics.

Friendship Caravan
U.S. students travel through Australia, the Commonwealth of Independent States, or the United Kingdom, visiting major cities and small towns.

SELECTION PROCESS

Outbound students must complete an application form and interview questionnaire, along with three letters of recommendation. Local educators and business leaders will form an interview committee to screen students. Applications are accepted through the winter for the following year's programs. Some grants and interest-free loans will be available on a needs basis.

SUPPORT SERVICES

Students must attend 12 hours of orientation sessions before departure. Many programs also include two and one-half days of final orientation in Washington, D.C. Students receive a participation manual and orientation materials to help prepare for the trip. (Internships are available to past participants.) The accompanying escorts provide counseling support as needed.

PHENIX INTERNATIONAL CAMPUSES

The goal of Phenix International Campuses is to give young people opportunities for supervised travel in other countries, plus individual experiences in homestays. The homestay offers every student one-on-one contact with people in another culture. It has proved to be more important than the travel. Students learn the language quickly. They learn to appreciate another culture while making lifelong friends. They also learn a great deal about themselves and, by comparison, their own culture.

Contact: Nellie B. Jackson, Director
7651 North Carolyn Drive
Castle Rock, CO 80104

Telephone: 303/688-9397
Fax: 303/688-6543

Non-profit corporation (1970)

Destinations: France, Germany, Mexico, Russia, Spain

100 students outbound from the United States
60 students inbound to the United States

PROGRAM DESCRIPTIONS

Treasures of France
U.S. students travel to France to live with screened host families and tour historic and cultural sites.

Espana es su Casa
U.S. students travel to Spain to live with screened host families and tour historic and cultural sites.

Modern and Historic Mexico
U.S. students travel to Mexico to live with screened host families and tour historic and cultural sites.

Adventures in Germany
U.S. students travel to Germany to live with screened host families and tour historic and cultural sites.

The Soviet Union Today
U.S. students travel to Russia to live with screened host families and tour historic and cultural sites.

PHENIX INTERNATIONAL CAMPUSES				
Programs	Length of Stay	Ages Served	Approximate Fee	Requirements
Treasures of France	22 days	Junior high and high school students	$2,989, including transportation and insurance	1 year of training in French
Espana es su Casa	24 days	Junior high and high school students	$2,889, including transportation and insurance	1 year of training in Spanish
Modern and Historic Mexico	17 days	Junior high and high school students	$1,169, including transportation and insurance	1 year of training in Spanish
Adventures in Germany	22 days	Junior high and high school students	$2,789, including transportation and insurance	1 year of training in German
The Soviet Union Today	21 days	Junior high and high school students	$2,990, including transportation and insurance	1 year of training in Russian

SELECTION PROCESS

Outbound students submit an application; then, Phenix requests references from teachers and counselors. After approval, Phenix requires additional records such as medical forms.

Host families of inbound students submit an application, followed by an interview with Phenix representatives.

SUPPORT SERVICES

Phenix supplies an extensive pre-departure orientation. Trained counselors and chaperones conduct the programs in each host country. Local representatives make host family arrangements and assist during the homestay.

PROAMERICAN EDUCATIONAL AND CULTURAL EXCHANGE

PEACE emphasizes academic-year programs for U.S. and Latin American high school students. PEACE believes that only through long-term immersion can a student gain fluency in another language, become functional in a different culture, and make deep-lasting relationships. PEACE hopes to lower racial and ethnic barriers across national borders.

Contact: Richard S. Page, Executive Director
40 Water Street, Suite 700
New Philadelphia, PA 17959

              Telephone: 800/377-2232
                                717/277-6621
              Fax: 717/277-0607

Non-profit corporation (1988)

Destinations: Bolivia, Brazil, Colombia, Ecuador, Mexico, Panama, Peru, Venezuela

              10 students outbound from the United States
              100 students inbound to the United States

PROMERICAN EDUCATIONAL AND CULTURAL EXCHANGE				
Programs	Length of Stay	Ages Served	Approximate Fee	Requirements
Academic Year Program	1 academic quarter, semester, or year	High school students	$2,200 (quarter), $2,850 (semester), or $3,500 (year), including transportation [U.S. students only]	A minimum of 2 years of classroom instruction in the host language

PROGRAM DESCRIPTIONS

Academic Year Program

U.S. students live with screened host families and attend high school. (Private schools are available, but additional tuition fees may be required.)

International students live with screened U.S. host families and attend high school. (Private schools are available, but additional tuition fees may be required.)

SELECTION PROCESS

Outbound students complete an application form and a $50 fee for language tests. Then, students and their parents are interviewed in the home. After the interview, students complete a medical questionnaire and an academic history form; they also submit evaluations from their language teachers and other school and community references. The deadline is April 1 for fall enrollment and September 1 for winter enrollment.

Host families of inbound students complete an application form and submit five references. Personal interviews are then conducted in the home. Host families must follow the Christian faith.

PEACE sponsors two students each year on merit scholarships, waiving all fees except transportation and insurance expenses.

SUPPORT SERVICES

PEACE conducts pre-departure and post-arrival orientation sessions. Professional counselors provide in-home counseling as needed. Students and host families receive handbooks and other written materials. A 24-hour emergency number is available to students and host families.

ROTARY INTERNATIONAL EXCHANGE PROGRAMS

With more than 25,000 clubs in 172 countries, Rotary International operates one of the world's largest youth exchange programs, almost entirely with volunteers. Rotary commits more than 30 years of sponsoring successful international exchanges to give future students an exchange experience filled with personal growth and warm memories.

Contact: Alison O'Brien, Youth Exchange Program Coordinator
1560 Sherman Avenue
Evanston, IL 60201

Telephone: 708/866-3421
Fax: 708/328-8554

Non-profit corporation (1972)

Destinations: Argentina, Australia, Austria, Bahamas, Bangladesh, Belgium, Bermuda, Bolivia, Brazil, Canada, Chile, Colombia, Costa Rica, Croatia, Czech Republic, Denmark, Dominican Republic, Ecuador, Faroe Islands, Finland, France, Germany, Greece, Greenland, Haiti, Hungary, Iceland, India, Indonesia, Israel, Italy, Japan, Latvia, Lithuania, Luxembourg, Malaysia, Mexico, Netherlands, New Caledonia, New Zealand, Norway, People's Republic of China, Peru, Phillipines, Poland, Portugal, Romania, Russia, Slovakia, Slovenia, South Africa, Spain, Swaziland, Sweden, Switzerland, Thailand, Turkey, Ukraine, United Kingdom, Uruguay, Venezuela, Yugoslavia, Zimbabwe
NOTE: Rotarians in approximately 400 districts around the world operate independent, autonomous exchange programs. Individual districts and clubs may or may not operate programs in all of the nations named above.

2,256 students outbound from the United States
2,737 students inbound to the United States

PROGRAM DESCRIPTIONS

Through its global network of more than 26,000 clubs in 187 countries, Rotary International facilitates exchange programs within individual districts; it does not serve as a direct sponsor of youth exchanges.

Generally, Rotary exchanges involve U.S. and international students ages 15 to 19 who are recommended and sponsored by a Rotary club or district. Students complete application forms and take part in personal interviews to be selected for the program. The sending district arranges orientations for exchange students and parents; also, that district finalizes arrangements for a host family in the receiving Rotary district. Each student pays round-trip transportation and insurance costs; other expenses will be paid by the host family and the receiving district. The receiving district also coordinates post-arrival orientation sessions, introductions to the local high school, and a modest monthly stipend for the student. When students return from the exchange, they should plan to attend re-entry sessions in their home district.

Because Rotary exchange programs vary from district to district, prospective students and host families should contact their local Rotary club or the international office in Evanston, Ill., for complete details.

SCHOOL YEAR ABROAD

Since 1964, more than 2,500 students from 500 secondary school have taken advantage of this unique opportunity to become comfortable and competent in another culture, while pursuing a demanding academic program that guarantees full U.S. academic credit and preparation for top U.S. colleges. Students gain self- confidence and maturity, along with language mastery and international awareness.

Parent organization: Phillips Academy

Contact: W.W. Halsey II, Executive Director
Phillips Academy
180 Main St.
Andover, MA 01810
Telephone: 508/749-4420
Fax: 508/749-4425
Non-profit organization (1975)

Destinations: France, Spain
119 students outbound from the United States

PROGRAM DESCRIPTIONS

School Year Abroad
U.S. students live with screened host families in France or Spain and follow a very rigorous curriculum at an SYA center: at least three

SCHOOL YEAR ABROAD				
Programs	Length of Stay	Ages Served	Approximate Fee	Requirements
School Year Abroad	8½ months	High school juniors and seniors	SYA fees are competitive with U.S. boarding school fees and include tuition, room and board, and excursions for all days abroad (including vacations); however, the fees do not include international transportation.	Successful students must demonstrate strong grades, above-average language ability, proven motivation, and excellent "ambassadorial" skills.

courses taught exclusively in French or Spanish, as well as core classes in math and English. The program also includes organized excursions and extracurricular activities.

SELECTION PROCESS

Outbound students must undergo an extremely competitive process to be selected for SYA's programs. They file an application with four confidential recommendations, school transcripts, personal essays, and a "Dear Family" letter to the hosts. SYA staffers in Andover or local SYA alumni near the student's home will conduct a personal interview.

More than one-third of the students receive scholarships and grants (average award: $13,330).

SUPPORT SERVICES

SYA sends printed orientation materials to students before departure. Group orientation exercises will begin in the host country after arrival. SYA offers academic testing (PSAT, SAT, ACT, AP) and college counseling throughout the year.

VISTAS IN EDUCATION

Vistas in Education is a travel arranger dedicated to providing exceptional travel and family stay programs in France for American students and their teachers.

Contact: Jane Weinstein, Program Director
1422 West Lake Street
Minneapolis, MN 55408

Telephone: 612/823-7217
Fax: 612/823-9064

For-profit corporation (1976)

Destinations: France

1,000 students outbound from the United States
300 students inbound to the United States

PROGRAM DESCRIPTIONS

Travel and Family Stay Programs

U.S. students combine a one-week homestay with screened French host families with a selected tour of historic and cultural sites in France.

SELECTION PROCESS

Outbound students must have the recommendations of their teachers and complete a registration form and a "Dear Family" letter to the hosts.

Host families of inbound students complete an application, listing two references and the student's language teacher. Families will then be interviewed.

SUPPORT SERVICES

Students and host families receive handbooks and attend orientation sessions. Chaperones and on-call counselors provide assistance as needed.

VISTAS IN EDUCATION				
Programs	Length of Stay	Ages Served	Approximate Fee	Requirements
Travel and Family Stay Programs	10 days, 15 days, or 22 days	High school students	Fees range from $995 to $2,045, depending upon length of stay and U.S. departure city and including transportation.	U.S. teachers accompanying groups of students must be fluent in French.

WO INTERNATIONAL CENTER

The Wo International Center provides opportunities for challenging international experiences, lending a global perspective to learning. Opportunities are available for intensive study abroad for Hawaiian, mainland, and international students at the secondary level. The focus is on foreign language and culture studies, including a stay with host families. As an introduction to other cultures, these programs serve as a catalyst towards international understanding.

Contact: Siegfried Ramler, Director
1601 Punahou Street
Honolulu, HI 96822

Telephone: 808/944-5871
Fax: 808/944-5712

Academic affiliate (1968)
Parent organization: Punahou School

Destinations: French Polynesia, Germany, Japan, People's Republic of China, Russia

100 students outbound from the United States
43 students inbound to the United States

PROGRAM DESCRIPTIONS

Study in China
U.S. students live in the guest house of Beijing's Capital Normal University during the summer. They study Mandarin Chinese and take part in organized field trips in the Beijing area. Following the four-week Beijing stay, they spend two weeks visiting major cultural sites in China, returning via Hong Kong.

Study in Japan
U.S. students live with screened host families and study Japanese language and civilization during the summer. The program is conducted at Tokyo's Keio School and, in alternate years, at the Katoh Schools in Numazu. Students participate in planned excursions and visit major cultural sites in Japan.

WO INTERNATIONAL CENTER				
Programs	Length of Stay	Ages Served	Approximate Fee	Requirements
Study in China	6 weeks	Grades 9 through 12	$3,500, including transportation	None
Study in Japan	4 weeks	Grades 9 through 12	$3,400, including transportation	None
Study in Tahiti	5 weeks	Grades 9 through 12	$3,000, including transportation	While proficiency in French is not required, it will be helpful.
Study in Russia	6 weeks	Grades 11 and 12	Approximately $3,300, including transportation	None
Study in Germany	6 weeks	Grades 9 through 12	Approximately $3,000, including transportation	While proficiency in German is not required, it will be helpful.
Pan Pacific Program in the United States	5 weeks	Grades 9 through 12	$2,500, excluding transportation	A background of English language study, equivalent to 3 to 4 years of high school classes

Study in Tahiti

U.S. students live with screened host families and take classes in a local secondary school. They study French language and civilization and Polynesian culture. Visits to Moorea and other islands are included.

Study in Russia

U.S. students live with screened host families in Magadan, a port city on the Pacific Ocean north of Vladivostok. They study Russian language and culture, take cultural excursions, and participate in extracurricular activities. After four weeks in Magadan, the students tour Moscow and St. Petersburg for two weeks.

Study in Germany

U.S. students live with screened host families and study German language and culture at a local secondary school (in conjunction with the German-American Partnership Program). Reciprocal hosting of a German student in Hawaii is expected. The program includes travel to various parts of Germany.

In turn, U.S. students agree to host a German student in their homes.

Pan Pacific Program in the United States

Students from French Polynesia, Germany, Japan, and China live with Hawaiian host families in the summer. The program provides intensive study of the English language and American culture at Honolulu's Punahou School and includes planned excursions. One weeks is spent in Kamuela on the island of Hawaii.

SELECTION PROCESS

While outbound students come mainly from schools in Hawaii, students from the U.S. mainland are also accepted. Students complete an application form and supply references, recommendation letters, and school transcripts. A selection committee interviews each student.

SUPPORT SERVICES

Wo International Center staffers provide pre- departure orientation sessions for seven to 10 days in Honolulu. Faculty chaperones accompany students to the host country and serve as counselors during the trip.

WORLD EDUCATIONAL SERVICES FOUNDATION

WES Foundation is an educational institution dedicated to the promotion of world understanding through cultural exchange between the United States and other nations. WES Foundation is a designated sponsor of a Teenager-Exchange-Visitor Program by the U.S. Information Agency. The WES program is designed for students 15 to 18 years of age.

Contact: Manuel Cabello, President
2201 Broadway, Suite 101
Oakland, CA 94612-3023

Telephone: 510/452-0200
Fax: 510/452-9430

Non-profit corporation (1982)

Destinations: Brazil, Chile, Ecuador, Hong Kong, Japan, Spain

5 students outbound from the United States
250 students inbound to the United States

WORLD EDUCATIONAL SERVICES FOUNDATION				
Programs	Length of Stay	Ages Served	Approximate Fee	Requirements
Semester/Academic Year Abroad Program	1 semester or academic year	15 to 18	$3,500 to $4,500 (semester) or $5,500 to $7,000 (year), excluding transportation	None
Semester/Academic Year Program in the United States	1 semester or academic year	15 to 18	$3,500 (semester) or $4,500 (year), excluding transportation; no fee for host families	Basic proficiency in English

PROGRAM DESCRIPTIONS

Semester/Academic Year Abroad Program

U.S. students live with screened host families and attend classes in the local high school.

Semester/Academic Year Program in the United States

International students live with screened U.S. host families and attend classes in the local high school.

SELECTION PROCESS

Outbound students complete an application form, along with faculty recommendations, a medical history, school transcripts, and an essay. In addition, students must interview with WESF staffers and earn acceptable scores on a language proficiency test. The deadline is March 30 for programs which begin the following August.

Host families of inbound students complete an application form and then are interviewed by the local WESF coordinator. The deadline is five weeks before the student's arrival, or the first week in July for August programs.

SUPPORT SERVICES

WESF personnel conduct pre-departure and post-arrival orientation sessions for students. Students also receive a written manual for reference. Local WESF coordinators provide counseling as needed.

WORLD EXPERIENCE

World Experience offers teenagers a host family/school living experience in another country, to strengthen international ties through personally guided exchange programs.

Contact: Bobby Jean Fraker, President and CEO
2440 South Hacienda Blvd., Suite 116
Hacienda Heights, CA 91745

Telephone: 818/330-5719
Fax: 818/333-4914

Non-profit corporation (1977)

Destinations: Australia, Brazil, Bulgaria, Canada, Chile, Colombia, Czech Republic, Denmark, Ecuador, Estonia, Finland, France, Germany, Hungary, Japan, Mexico, New Zealand, Panama, Poland, Russia, Thailand, Uruguay, Venezuela

25 students outbound from the United States
216 students inbound to the United States

P R O G R A M   D E S C R I P T I O N S

Homestay/Study
U.S. students live with screened host families and attend classes in the local secondary school. As an option, students may earn independent study credit through WE's link with Eastern Washington University.

Summer Language Courses
U.S. students complete an intensive language program in Japan, Russia, or Spain. In Japan and Spain, students live with screened host

WORLD EXPERIENCE				
Programs	Length of Stay	Ages Served	Approximate Fee	Requirements
Homestay/ Study	1 semester or aca- demic year	15 to 18	$2,240 to $3,600 (semester) or $2,900 to $4,700 (year), excluding transportation; no fee for host families	Students traveling to France, Germany, or Spain must demonstrate a working knowledge of the host language.
Summer Language Courses	4 weeks	15 to 18	$1,215 to $2,585, excluding transportation	None

families; in Russia, the program begins with a one-week homestay, followed by a stay at a language camp north of Moscow.

SELECTION PROCESS

Outbound students complete an application form, including faculty recommendations and school transcripts.

WE offers scholarships and other forms of financial aid. Contact WE for details.

Host families of inbound students complete an application form; then, local WE volunteers interview each family in the home.

SUPPORT SERVICES

Students participate in pre-departure and post-arrival orientation sessions.

WORLD HERITAGE

World Heritage is a not-for-profit, public-benefit organization dedicated to fostering cultural enrichment and intercultural understanding through youth exchange programs. Founded in 1971 as Spanish Heritage, World Heritage continues to focus on Hispanic culture which holds such influence in North America, while at the same time expanding its programs to embrace other nationalities.

Also known as Spanish Heritage.

Contact: Michelle L. Garcia, Director
1288 1/2 31st Street, NW, Suite 5
Washington, DC 20007

Telephone: 202/625-6993
Fax: 202/625-6914

Non-profit corporation (1971)

Destinations: Canada, France, Mexico, Spain

134 students outbound from the United States
2,263 students inbound to the United States

WORLD HERITAGE				
Programs	Length of Stay	Ages Served	Approximate Fee	Requirements
Academic Summer/ Year Program	6 weeks or 10 months	15 to 18	$2,300 (summer) or $3,450 to $4,600 (year), including transportation and insurance	A grade-point average of at least B
Language Adventure	4 weeks	15 to 18	$2,600, including insurance and transportation	None

PROGRAM DESCRIPTIONS

Academic Summer/Year Program

U.S. students live with screened host families. On the year program, students attend classes in the local high school.

World Heritage can arrange reciprocal exchanges, so that returning U.S. students can provide a home for a student from their host country.

Language Adventure

U.S. students live with screened host families and take part in intensive language and cultural classes each morning, with organized activities in the evenings and on weekends to expose them to the host culture.

SELECTION PROCESS

Outbound students submit an application form, a "Dear Family" letter to the hosts, and recommendations from a community leader, a school administrator, and two teachers. In addition, the student must supply school transcripts and take part in an interview.

Host families of inbound students complete an application form and furnish three recommendations. A World Heritage representative will interview each family in the home.

SUPPORT SERVICES

Students and families receive orientation handbooks from World Heritage. Host families take part in orientation sessions conducted by area representatives. Students undergo orientation once they arrive in the host country. Area representatives monitor students' progress and provide counseling as needed.

WORLD LEARNING

Founded in 1932 as the U.S. Experiment in International Living, World Learning promotes international understanding through citizen exchange, language instruction, and projects in international development and training. Its academic arm, the School for International Training, offers undergraduate degrees in world studies and world issues, as well as graduate degrees in intercultural management and teaching English as a second language.

Also known as The U.S. Experiment in International Living.

Contact: Dr. Christine S. Burbach, Vice President
Kipling Road, POB 676
Brattleboro, VT 05302-0676

Telephone: 802/257-7751
Fax: 802/258-3248

Non-profit corporation (1932)

Destinations: Argentina, Australia, Austria, Belgium, Belize, Bolivia, Botswana, Brazil, Cameroon, Chile, Colombia, Czech Republic, Denmark, Dominican Republic, Ecuador, France, Germany, Greece, Guinea, Hong Kong, India, Indonesia, Ireland, Italy, Jamaica, Japan, Kenya, Madagascar, Mexico, Morocco, Nepal, Nigeria, Portugal, Russia, St. Vincent and the Grenadines, South Africa, Spain, Switzerland, Taiwan, Tanzania, Thailand, Turkey, United Kingdom, Venezuela, Vietnam, Western Samoa, Zimbabwe

1,505 students outbound from the United States
4,179 students inbound to the United States

PROGRAM DESCRIPTIONS

Summer Abroad

The Summer Abroad programs offer U.S. students a selection of homestay, travel, language training, ecological adventure, and community service components. These programs range from working in a kibbutz and exploring the desert by camelback in Israel to studying the ecology of Ecuador's Galapagos Islands.

International High School Program/
Congress-Bundestag Youth Exchange Program

U.S. students live with screened host families in Germany and attend public high schools.

International students live with screened host families and attend public high schools in the United States.

Youth Adventure Camp

International students spend 25 hours weekly in English language classes and participate in organized sports and excursions to Florida attractions.

Homestay/USA

International students live with screened host families and attend formal language classes for 12 hours weekly. The program also offers excursions to local attractions and events. Concentrations in arts and basketball are also available.

World Learning also offers programs for au pairs and for college students and older people who seek intensive English training.

WORLD LEARNING				
Programs	Length of Stay	Ages Served	Approximate Fee	Requirements
Summer Abroad	3 to 6 weeks	High school students	$2,000 to $2,500, including international transportation (except Mexico) and insurance	For programs to Spain, France, and Mexico, students must demonstrate proficiency in the host language.
International High School Program/ Congress Bundestag Youth Exchange Program	1 semester or academic year	15 to 18	International High School Program fees range from $2,000 to $2,700, including transportation and insurance. Because all costs are covered by U.S. and German grants, there is no fee for the Congress-Bundestag program (except domestic U.S. transportation) for qualified students.	Contact World Learning for full details.
Youth Adventure Camp	1 or 2 4-week sessions	11 to 15	$2,150, excluding international transportation	None
Homestay/USA	4 weeks	13 to 21	$1,050 to $1,300, excluding international transportation	None

SELECTION PROCESS

For the Summer Abroad programs, outbound students must complete an information sheet, a physician's approval form, a letter to the host family, and a membership conditions form. No interviews are required. Extensive scholarships ($500,000 to 200 students) based on need and merit are available. The application deadline is May 1.

For the International High School Program/Congress-Bundestag Youth Exchange Program, the selection process is very competitive. Contact World Learning for more details.

For the Youth Adventure Camp, students complete an application form. They may be accompanied by group leaders from their host country.

For the Homestay/USA Program, students apply through a World Learning representative in their host country. Interviews and recommendations may be required. The completed application must be filed at least six weeks before the program begins. Local U.S. coordinators screen and select volunteer host families, who fill out a family description form and complete a host family orientation session.

SUPPORT SERVICES

To prepare students and host families, World Learning presents multi-day orientation sessions, multi-day cross-cultural manuals, and local community and national staffers to monitor students and provide counseling as needed.

YOUTH EXCHANGE SERVICE

In a world of constant tension, YES has achieved through the international students a better understanding and respect among people. Overall, it has accomplished better communications through friendly relations between the United States and students around the world. This is a very special part of the great socio- economic sphere in which we live.

Contact: Leonardo Flores, President
4675 MacArthur Court, Suite 830
Newport Beach, CA 92660

Telephone: 800/848-2121
714/955-2030
Fax: 714/955-0232

YOUTH EXCHANGE SERVICE				
Programs	Length of Stay	Ages Served	Approximate Fee	Requirements
School Year Abroad	1 aca-demic year	15 to 18	$3,500, excluding transporta-tion; reduced fees are available to U.S. students who agree to host an international student	None
Overseas Semester to the United States	5 months	15 to 18	$2,300, including insurance but excluding transportation; no fee for host families	A working knowledge of English
Overseas Year to the United States	10 months	15 to 18	$3,200, including insurance but excluding transportation; no fee for host families	A working knowledge of English

Non-profit corporation (1974)

Destinations: Argentina, Belgium, Brazil, Colombia, Denmark, Ecuador, El Salvador, France, Germany, Hong Kong, Japan, Luxembourg, Mexico, Norway, Panama, Peru, Spain, Switzerland, Thailand, Venezuela, Zaire

10 students outbound from the United States
500 students inbound to the United States

PROGRAM DESCRIPTIONS

School Year Abroad
U.S. students live with screened host families and attend classes in the local high school.

Overseas Semester to the United States
International students live with screened U.S. host families and attend classes in the local high school.

Overseas Year to the United States
International students live with screened U.S. host families and attend classes in the local high school.

SELECTION PROCESS

Outbound students complete an application form and medical form and submit a school transcript, personal statement, and reference letters.

Host families of inbound students complete an application form and submit reference letters.

Students and host families receive exchange handbooks. Also, they participate in pre-departure and post-arrival orientation sessions.

YOUTH FOR UNDERSTANDING INTERNATIONAL EXCHANGE

YFU is a private, non-profit, educational organization dedicated to international understanding and world peace. YFU carries out one of the world's oldest, largest, and most respected international youth exchange programs. Established in 1951, more than 150,000 high school students have participated in YFU exchanges. Each year, about 4,000 international students come to the United States from 30 countries. YFU has a network of 10 regional offices in the United States and 30 national offices around the world.

Contact: Karen Yoho, Manager of Public Relations
3501 Newark Street, NW
Washington, DC 20016

Telephone: 800/424-3691
202/966-6800
Fax: 202/895-1104

Non-profit corporation (1951)

Destinations: Argentina, Australia, Belgium, Brazil, Chile, Colombia, Commonwealth of Independent States, Czech Republic, Denmark, Ecuador, Finland, France, Germany, Greece, Hungary, Italy, Japan, Korea, Latvia, Mexico, Netherlands, New Zealand, Norway, Paraguay, People's Republic of China, Phillipines, Poland, Russia, Spain, Sweden, Switzerland, United Kingdom, Uruguay, Venezuela

2,281 students outbound from the United States
3,780 students inbound to the United States

PROGRAM DESCRIPTIONS

American Overseas Summer Program
U.S. students live with screened host families, participating in family and community activities.

American Overseas Semester Program

U.S. students live with screened host families and attend classes in the local high school.

American Overseas Year Program

U.S. students live with screened host families and attend classes in the local high school.

Sport for Understanding

U.S. students travel in teams to play one of 12 selected sports in another country. In most cases, they live as a team in one location, with planned excursions to play host teams in other cities. They are led by volunteer coaches and hosted by sports clubs, coaches, and local families.

YOUTH FOR UNDERSTANDING				
Programs	Length of Stay	Ages Served	Approximate Fee	Requirements
American Overseas Summer Program	2 months	15 to 18	$2,040 to $3,290, including international transportation	Students traveling to Belgium, Chile, France, Spain, Switzerland, or Venezuela must demonstrate prior knowledge of the host language.
American Overseas Semester Program	1 semester	15 to 18	$4,075 to $5,215, including international transportation	Students traveling to Belgium, Chile, France, Spain, Switzerland, or Venezuela must demonstrate prior knowledge of the host language.
American Overseas Year Program	1 academic year	15 to 18	$4,370 to $5,530, including international transportation	Students traveling to Belgium, Chile, France, Spain, Switzerland, or Venezuela must demonstrate prior knowledge of the host language.
Sport for Understanding	4 weeks	14 to 19	$2,450 to $2,875, including international transportation	None
International Semester to the United States	1 semester	15 to 18	$3,500 to $5,500, including international transportation; no fee for host families	Proficiency in English
International Year to the United States	1 academic year	15 to 18	$3,500 to $8,500, including international transportation; no fee for host families	Proficiency in English

International Semester to the United States
International students live with screened U.S. host families and attend classes in the local high school.

International Year to the United States
International students live with screened U.S. host families and attend classes in the local high school.

SELECTION PROCESS

Outbound students complete an application form, medical and dental forms, and a letter to the host family; also, they submit school transcripts, faculty recommendations, and proof of insurance. Then, they will be interviewed by YFU personnel. The deadline is April 1 for programs which begin in the summer or fall.

YFU offers a very comprehensive range of scholarships. Financial Aid awards will be given on the basis of need. YFU administers two scholarship programs funded by the governments of the United States, Finland, and Germany. More than 330 merit-based scholarships for the summer program and four scholarships for the year program are available for students whose parents work for one of 60 sponsoring corporations (and, in many cases, for students who live in a community in which the corporation operates). Finally, three scholarships have been established by private donors for students going to Germany.

Host families of inbound students submit an application form, a host family agreement, and two references. In addition, each family will be interviewed in the home by YFU personnel. The deadline is July 1 for programs which begin in the summer or fall.

SUPPORT SERVICES

YFU conducts orientation sessions for students. Handbooks are provided to students and their parents and to host families. Trained YFU volunteers and staffers offer counseling in the host country as needed. YFU sponsors "returnee" sessions to assist students in making the transition home after the exchange ends.

Exchange Programs by Country

ARGENTINA

AFS Intercultural Programs
ASPECT Foundation
Center for Cultural Interchange
Children's International Summer Villages
Educational Resource Development Trust
International Student Exchange of Iowa
Open Door Student Exchange
Rotary International Exchange Programs
World Learning
Youth Exchange Service
Youth for Understanding

AUSTRALIA

Academic and Cultural Exchange
AFS Intercultural Programs
American Intercultural Student Exchange
American International Youth Student Exchange Program
American Secondary Schools for International Students and Teachers
ASSE International Student Exchange
AYUSA International

Children's International Summer Villages
Creative Response
Cultural Homestay International
International Christian Youth Exchange
International Education Forum
International Travel Study
National FFA Program
Open Door Student Exchange
People to People High School Student Ambassador Program
Rotary International Exchange Programs
World Experience
World Learning
Youth for Understanding

A U S T R I A

AFS Intercultural Programs
American Intercultural Student Exchange
Amicus International Youth Student Exchange Program
ASPECT Foundation
Children's International Summer Villages
Cultural Homestay International
Foreign Study League
International Christian Youth Exchange
International Education Forum
INTRAX—International Training and Exchange
National Association of Secondary School Principals, School
    Partnerships, International
People to People High School Student Ambassador Program
Rotary International Exchange Programs
World Learning

B A H A M A S

Rotary International Exchange Programs

B A L T I C   S T A T E S
(ESTONIA, LATVIA, LITHUANIA)

AFS Intercultural Programs
American Secondary Schools for International Students and Teachers
AYUSA International
Creative Response
Open Door Student Exchange
People to People High School Student Ambassador Program
Rotary International Exchange Programs

World Experience
Youth for Understanding

BANGLADESH

Rotary International Exchange Programs

BELGIUM

Academic and Cultural Exchange
AFS Intercultural Programs
American Intercultural Student Exchange
American International Youth Student Exchange Program
American Secondary Schools for International Students and Teachers
ASPECT Foundation
AYUSA International
Children's International Summer Villages
Creative Response
Cultural Homestay International
Educational Resource Development Trust
International Christian Youth Exchange
International Education Forum
Rotary International Exchange Programs
World Learning
Youth Exchange Service
Youth for Understanding

BELIZE

World Learning

BERMUDA

Rotary International Programs Exchange

BOLIVIA

AFS Intercultural Programs
Iberoamerican Cultural Exchange Program
International Christian Youth Exchange
International Student Exchange
Open Door Student Exchange
ProAmerican Educational and Cultural Exchange
Rotary International Exchange Programs
World Learning

BOTSWANA

World Learning

BRAZIL

Academic and Cultural Exchange
AFS Intercultural Programs
American Intercultural Student Exchange
American International Youth Student Exchange Program
Amigos de las Americas
ASPECT Foundation
AYUSA International
Children's International Summer Villages
Creative Response
Cultural Homestay International
Educational Resource Development Trust
Foundation for International Understanding
International Christian Youth Exchange
International Education Forum
International Student Exchange
International Travel Study
Legacy International
Open Door Student Exchange
PACE Institute International
ProAmerican Educational and Cultural Exchange
Rotary International Exchange Programs
World Educational Services Foundation
World Experience
World Learning
Youth Exchange Service
Youth for Understanding

BULGARIA

American Secondary Schools for International Students and Teachers
AYUSA International
Children's International Summer Villages
International Travel Study
National FFA Organization
Open Door Student Exchange
World Experience

CAMEROON

World Learning

CANADA

AFS Intercultural Programs
American International Youth Student Exchange Program
Children's International Summer Villages
Creative Response
Cultural Homestay International
Intercambio Internacional de Estudiantes
International Education Forum
International Travel Study
Legacy International
National Association of Secondary School Principals, School
    Partnerships, International
Open Door Student Exchange
Rotary International Exchange Programs
World Experience
World Heritage

CANARY ISLANDS

ASPECT Foundation

CHILE

AFS Intercultural Programs
American International Youth Student Exchange Program
Children's International Summer Villages
Open Door Student Exchange
Rotary International Exchange Programs
World Educational Services Foundation
World Experience
World Learning
Youth for Understanding

COLOMBIA

AFS Intercultural Programs
American Intercultural Student Exchange
ASPECT Foundation
AYUSA International
Cultural Homestay International
International Christian Youth Exchange
International Education Forum
International Student Exchange
Legacy International
Open Door Student Exchange
Pacific Intercultural Exchange
ProAmerican Educational and Cultural Exchange

Rotary International Exchange Programs
World Experience
World Learning
Youth Exchange Service
Youth for Understanding

COMMONWEALTH OF INDEPENDENT STATES
(BYELORUS, GEORGIA, KAZAKHSTAN, RUSSIA, THE UKRAINE, AND OTHER PARTS OF THE FORMER U.S.S.R.)

Academic and Cultural Exchange
AFS Intercultural Programs
ASPECT Foundation
AYUSA International
Children's International Summer Villages
Council on International Educational Exchange—School Partners
    Abroad
Creative Response
Cultural Homestay International
Educational Resource Development Trust
Foreign Study League
International Education Forum
International Travel Study
Legacy International
National Association of Secondary School Principals, School
    Partnerships, International
Open Door Student Exchange
People to People High School Student Ambassador Program
Phenix International Campuses
Rotary International Exchange Programs
Wo International Center
World Experience
World Learning
Youth for Understanding

COSTA RICA

AFS Intercultural Programs
Amigos de las Americas
Children's International Summer Villages
Council on International Educational Exchange—School Partners
    Abroad
Creative Response
Iberoamerican Cultural Exchange Program

Intercambio Internacional de Estudiantes
International Christian Youth Exchange
International Education Forum
Legacy International
National Association of Secondary School Principals, School
    Partnerships, International
National FFA Organization
Open Door Student Exchange
People to People High School Student Ambassador Program
Rotary International Exchange Programs

CZECH REPUBLIC AND SLOVAKIA

AFS Intercultural Programs
American Intercultural Student Exchange
American International Youth Student Exchange Program
ASPECT Foundation
AYUSA International
Children's International Summer Villages
Creative Response
Cultural Homestay International
Educational Resource Development Trust
International Education Forum
International Travel Study
INTRAX—International Training and Learning
Legacy International
Open Door Student Exchange
People to People High School Student Ambassador Program
Rotary International Exchange Programs
World Experience
World Learning
Youth for Understanding

DENMARK

AFS Intercultural Programs
American Intercultural Student Exchange
American International Youth Student Exchange Program
American Secondary Schools for International Students
    and Teachers
ASPECT Foundation
AYUSA International
Children's International Summer Villages
Cultural Homestay International
Educational Resource Development Trust
International Christian Youth Exchange

International Education Forum
INTRAX—International Training and Exchange
Open Door Student Exchange
PACE Institute International
People to People High School Student Ambassador Program
Rotary International Exchange Programs
World Experience
World Learning
Youth Exchange Service
Youth for Understanding

DJIBOUTI

Legacy International

DOMINICAN REPUBLIC

AFS Intercultural Programs
Amigos de las Americas
Rotary International Exchange Programs
World Learning

EASTERN CARIBBEAN
(ANTIGUA, BARBADOS, GRENADA, ST. LUCIA, AND ST. VINCENT AND THE GRENADINES)

AFS Intercultural Programs
World Learning

ECUADOR

AFS Intercultural Programs
American Intercultural Student Exchange
Amigos de las Americas
ASPECT Foundation
Open Door Student Exchange
ProAmerican Educational and Cultural Exchange
Rotary International Exchange Programs
World Educational Services Foundation
World Experience
World Learning
Youth Exchange Service
Youth for Understanding

EGYPT

AFS Intercultural Programs
Children's International Summer Villages
International Education Forum
International Student Exchange
Open Door Student Exchange

EL SALVADOR

Children's International Summer Villages
Intercambio Internacional de Estudiantes
Youth Exchange Service

FAEROE ISLANDS

Children's International Summer Villages
Rotary International Exchange Programs

FINLAND

AFS Intercultural Programs
American Intercultural Student Exchange
American International Youth Student Exchange Program
ASPECT Foundation
Children's International Summer Villages
Cultural Homestay International
International Christian Youth Exchange
International Education Forum
PACE Institute International
People to People High School Student Ambassador Program
Rotary International Exchange Programs
World Experience
Youth for Understanding

FRANCE

AFS Intercultural Programs
American Intercultural Student Exchange
American International Youth Student Exchange Program
ASPECT Foundation
AYUSA International
Children's International Summer Villages
Council on International Educational Exchange—School Partners Abroad
Cultural Homestay International
De France
Educational Resource Development Trust
Foundation for International Understanding

International Christian Youth Exchange
International Education Forum
International Student Exchange
International Travel Study
INTRAX—International Training and Exchange
Legacy International
National Association of Secondary School Principals, School
Partnerships, International
Open Door Student Exchange
PACE Institute International
People to People High School Student Ambassador Program
Phenix International Campuses
Rotary International Exchange Programs
School Year Abroad
Vistas in Education
World Experience
World Heritage
World Learning
Youth Exchange Service
Youth for Understanding

FRENCH POLYNESIA

Wo International Center

GERMANY

Academic and Cultural Exchange
AFS Intercultural Programs
American Association of Teachers of German
American Intercultural Student Exchange
American International Youth Student Exchange Program
American Secondary Schools for International Students and
Teachers
ASPECT Foundation
AYUSA International
CDS International
Children's International Summer Villages
Council on International Educational Exchange—School Partners Abroad
Creative Response
Cultural Homestay International
Educational Resource Development Trust
Foreign Study League
International Christian Youth Exchange
International Education Forum
International Student Exchange
International Travel Study

INTRAX—International Training and Exchange
National Association of Secondary School Principals, School
    Partnerships, International
National FFA Organization
Open Door Student Exchange
PACE Institute International
People to People High School Student Ambassador Program
Phenix International Campuses
Rotary International Exchange Programs
Wo International Center
World Experience
World Learning
Youth Exchange Service
Youth for Understanding

GHANA

AFS Intercultural Programs
Cultural Homestay International
International Christian Youth Exchange
Legacy International

GREECE

American Farm School
Children's International Summer Villages
International Travel Study
National FFA Organization
Rotary International Exchange Programs
World Learning
Youth for Understanding

GREENLAND

Rotary International Exchange Programs

GUATEMALA

AFS Intercultural Programs
Casa de Espanol Xelaju
Children's International Summer Villages
Iberoamerican Cultural Exchange Program
Intercambio Internacional de Estudiantes

GUINEA

World Learning

HAITI

Rotary International Exchange Programs

HONDURAS

AFS Intercultural Programs
Amigos de las Americas
Children's International Summer Villages
International Christian Youth Exchange

HONG KONG

AFS Intercultural Programs
International Education Forum
People to People High School Student Ambassador Program
World Educational Services Foundation
World Learning
Youth Exchange Service

HUNGARY

Academic and Cultural Exchange
AFS Intercultural Programs
American Intercultural Student Exchange
American Secondary Schools for International Students and Teachers
AYUSA International
Children's International Summer Villages
Creative Response
International Education Forum
International Student Exchange
International Travel Study
INTRAX—International Training and Exchange
Legacy International
Open Door Student Exchange
People to People High School Student Ambassador Program
Rotary International Exchange Programs
World Experience
Youth for Understanding

ICELAND

AFS Intercultural Programs
Children's International Summer Villages
International Christian Youth Exchange
Rotary International Exchange Programs

I N D I A

American Secondary Schools for International Students and Teachers
Children's International Summer Villages
International Christian Youth Exchange
Rotary International Exchange Programs
World Learning

I N D O N E S I A

AFS Intercultural Programs
ASPECT Foundation
Creative Response
Open Door Student Exchange
Rotary International Exchange Programs
World Learning

I R E L A N D

American International Youth Student Exchange Program
Foreign Study League
International Travel Study
Irish Way
Legacy International
World Learning

I S R A E L

Children's International Summer Villages
Creative Response
Legacy International
Open Door Student Exchange
Rotary International Exchange Programs

I T A L Y

AFS Intercultural Programs
American Intercultural Student Exchange
American International Youth Student Exchange Program
ASPECT Foundation
AYUSA International
Children's International Summer Villages
Educational Resource Development Trust
International Christian Youth Exchange
International Education Forum
International Student Exchange
International Travel Study
INTRAX—International Training and Exchange

National Association of Secondary School Principals, School
     Partnerships, International
Open Door Student Exchange
PACE Institute International
Rotary International Exchange Programs
World Learning
Youth for Understanding

J A M A I C A

AFS Intercultural Programs
World Learning

J A P A N

AFS Intercultural Programs
American Intercultural Student Exchange
American International Youth Student Exchange Program
ASPECT Foundation
AYUSA International
Children's International Summer Villages
Council on International Educational Exchange—School Partners Abroad
Creative Response
Cultural Homestay International
Educational Resource Development Trust
Foundation for International Understanding
International Christian Youth Exchange
International Education Forum
International Student Exchange
Legacy International
National Association of Secondary School Principals, School
     Partnerships, International
National FFA Organization
Open Door Student Exchange
PACE Institute International
Rotary International Exchange Programs
Wo International Center
World Educational Services Foundation
World Experience
World Learning
Youth Exchange Service
Youth for Understanding

J O R D A N

Children's International Summer Villages

KENYA

Legacy International
World Learning

KOREA (SOUTH)

AFS Intercultural Programs
American Intercultural Student Exchange
ASPECT Foundation
Children's International Summer Villages
Creative Response
International Christian Youth Exchange
Legacy International
Youth for Understanding

LUXEMBOURG

Children's International Summer Villages
International Student Exchange
Rotary International Exchange Programs
Youth Exchange Service

MADAGASCAR

World Learning

MALAYSIA

AFS Intercultural Programs
Rotary International Exchange Programs

MEXICO

AFS Intercultural Programs
Amigos de las Americas
ASPECT Foundation
AYUSA International
Children's International Summer Villages
Educational Resource Development Trust
Foreign Study League
Iberoamerican Cultural Exchange Program
Intercambio Internacional de Estudiantes
International Christian Youth Exchange
International Education Forum
International Student Exchange
INTRAX—International Training and Exchange
Legacy International

National Association of Secondary School Principals, School
    Partnerships, International
Open Door Student Exchange
PACE Institute International
Phenix International Campuses
ProAmerican Educational and Cultural Exchange
Rotary International Exchange Programs
World Experience
World Heritage
World Learning
Youth Exchange Service
Youth for Understanding

M O N A C O

International Travel Study

M O N G O L I A

Children's International Summer Villages

M O R O C C O

Legacy International
World Learning

N E P A L

World Learning

N E T H E R L A N D S

AFS Intercultural Programs
American Intercultural Student Exchange
American International Youth Student Exchange Program
ASPECT Foundation
AYUSA International
Children's International Summer Villages
Creative Response
International Education Forum
International Travel Study
People to People High School Student Ambassador Program
Rotary International Exchange Programs
Youth for Understanding

N E W   C A L E D O N I A

Rotary International Exchange Programs

NEW ZEALAND

AFS Intercultural Programs
American Intercultural Student Exchange
American International Youth Student Exchange Program
AYUSA International
Children's International Summer Villages
Creative Response
Cultural Homestay International
International Christian Youth Exchange
PACE Institute International
People to People High School Student Ambassador Program
Rotary International Exchange Programs
World Experience
Youth for Understanding

NIGERIA

Children's International Summer Villages
Creative Response
International Christian Youth Exchange
Legacy International
World Learning

NORWAY

AFS Intercultural Programs
American Intercultural Student Exchange
American International Youth Student Exchange Program
ASPECT Foundation
Children's International Summer Villages
Educational Resource Development Trust
International Christian Youth Exchange
International Education Forum
International Student Exchange
PACE Institute International
Rotary International Exchange Programs
Youth Exchange Service
Youth for Understanding

PANAMA

AFS Intercultural Programs
Intercambio Internacional de Estudiantes
World Experience
Youth Exchange Service

PARAGUAY

AFS Intercultural Programs
Amigos de las Americas
ASPECT Foundation
Open Door Student Exchange
Youth for Understanding

PEOPLE'S REPUBLIC OF CHINA

AFS Intercultural Programs
Creative Response
Cultural Homestay International
International Student Exchange
People to People High School Student Ambassador Program
Rotary International Exchange Programs
Wo International Center
Youth for Understanding

PERU

AFS Intercultural Programs
American Intercultural Student Exchange
Iberoamerican Cultural Exchange Program
ProAmerican Educational and Cultural Exchange
Rotary International Exchange Programs
Youth for Understanding

PHILIPPINES

Children's International Summer Villages
Creative Response
Rotary International Exchange Programs
Youth for Understanding

POLAND

American Intercultural Student Exchange
ASPECT Foundation
AYUSA International
Children's International Summer Villages
Creative Response
Cultural Homestay International
International Christian Youth Exchange
International Education Forum
INTRAX—International Training and Exchange
Open Door Student Exchange
Pacific Intercultural Exchange

People to People High School Student Ambassador Program
Rotary International Exchange Programs
World Experience
Youth for Understanding

PORTUGAL

AFS Intercultural Programs
American International Youth Student Exchange Program
Children's International Summer Villages
International Education Forum
Rotary International Exchange Programs
World Learning

REUNION

Cultural Homestay International
International Education Forum

ROMANIA

American Secondary Schools for International Students
    and Teachers
AYUSA International
Children's International Summer Villages
International Education Forum
Open Door Student Exchange
PACE Institute International
Rotary International Exchange Programs

SENEGAL

Children's International Summer Villages
Legacy International

SIERRA LEONE

Children's International Summer Villages
International Christian Youth Exchange

SOUTH AFRICA

Creative Response
Rotary International Exchange Programs
World Learning

S P A I N

Academic and Cultural Exchange
AFS Intercultural Programs
American Intercultural Student Exchange
American International Youth Student Exchange Program
American Secondary Schools for International Students and Teachers
ASPECT Foundation
AYUSA International
Children's International Summer Villages
Council on International Educational Exchange—School Partners
    Abroad
Cultural Homestay International
Educational Resource Development Trust
Foreign Study League
Foundation for International Understanding
Iberoamerican Cultural Exchange Program
International Education Forum
International Student Exchange
International Travel Study
INTRAX—International Training and Exchange
Legacy International
National Association of Secondary School Principals, School
    Partnerships, International
Open Door Student Exchange
PACE Institute International
People to People High School Student Ambassador Program
Phenix International Campuses
Rotary International Exchange Programs
School Year Abroad
World Educational Services Foundation
World Heritage
World Learning
Youth Exchange Service
Youth for Understanding

S W A Z I L A N D

Rotary International Exchange Programs

S W E D E N

AFS Intercultural Programs
American Intercultural Student Exchange
American International Youth Student Exchange Program
American Secondary Schools for International Students and Teachers
ASPECT Foundation
AYUSA International

Children's International Summer Villages
Educational Resource Development Trust
International Christian Youth Exchange
International Education Forum
Open Door Student Exchange
PACE Institute International
People to People High School Student Ambassador Program
Rotary International Youth Exchange
Youth for Understanding

S W I T Z E R L A N D

AFS Intercultural Programs
American Intercultural Student Exchange
American International Youth Student Exchange Program
ASPECT Foundation
AYUSA International
Cultural Homestay International
Educational Resource Development Trust
International Christian Youth Exchange
International Travel Study
INTRAX—International Training and Exchange
PACE Institute International
People to People High School Student Ambassador Program
Rotary International Exchange Programs
World Learning
Youth Exchange Service
Youth for Understanding

T A I W A N

Cultural Homestay International
International Christian Youth Exchange
INTRAX—International Training and Exchange
PACE Institute International
World Learning

T A N Z A N I A

World Learning

T H A I L A N D

AFS Intercultural Programs
American Intercultural Student Exchange
AYUSA International
Children's International Summer Villages
Cultural Homestay International

Educational Resource Development Trust
International Education Forum
International Student Exchange
National FFA Organization
Open Door Student Exchange
PACE Institute International
Rotary International Exchange Programs
World Experience
World Learning
Youth Exchange Service

TURKEY

AFS Intercultural Programs
American Intercultural Student Exchange
Children's International Summer Villages
International Student Exchange
Legacy International
Rotary International Exchange Programs
World Learning

UNITED KINGDOM

AFS Intercultural Programs
American International Youth Student Exchange Program
ASPECT Foundation
AYUSA International
Children's International Summer Villages
Creative Response
International Travel Study
National Association of Secondary School Principals, School
    Partnerships, International
People to People High School Student Ambassador Program
Rotary International Exchange Programs
World Learning
Youth for Understanding

URUGUAY

Children's International Summer Villages
Open Door Student Exchange
Rotary International Exchange Programs
World Experience
Youth for Understanding

VATICAN CITY

International Travel Study

VENEZUELA

AFS Intercultural Programs
Legacy International
ProAmerican Educational and Cultural Exchange
Rotary International Exchange Programs
World Experience
World Learning
Youth Exchange Service
Youth for Understanding

VIETNAM

World Learning

YUGOSLAVIA
(CROATIA, MACEDONIA, AND SLOVENIA)

AFS Intercultural Programs
American Intercultural Student Exchange
American International Youth Student Exchange Program
ASPECT Foundation
AYUSA International
Children's International Summer Villages
Cultural Homestay International
Educational Resource Development Trust
International Education Forum
International Student Exchange
International Travel Study
INTRAX—International Training and Exchange
PACE Institute International
Rotary International Exchange Programs

ZAIRE

Youth Exchange Service

ZIMBABWE

Rotary International Exchange Programs
World Learning

APPENDIX B

U.S. Passport Agencies

Contact the nearest field office for complete details about applying for your passport. The 24-hour recording gives the office's hours of operation and location, as well as general passport information. Staffers will answer your questions on the public inquiries line during regular business hours.

Boston Passport Agency
Room 247, Thomas P. O'Neill
   Federal Bldg.
10 Causeway St.
Boston, MA 02222
Recording: 617/565-6998
Public inquiries: 617/565-6990

Chicago Passport Agency
Suite 380, Kluczynski Federal
   Bldg.
230 S. Dearborn St.
Chicago, IL 60604-1564
Recording: 312/353-7155

Honolulu Passport Agency
Room C-106, New Federal
   Bldg.
300 Ala Moana Blvd.
Honolulu, HI 96850
Recording: 808/541-1919
Public inquiries: 808/541-1918

Houston Passport Agency
Suite 1100, Mickey Leland
   Federal Bldg.
1919 Smith St.
Houston, TX 77002
Recording: 713/653-3153

Los Angeles Passport Agency
Room 13100, 11000 Wilshire
    Blvd.
Los Angeles, CA 90024-3615
Recording: 310/575-7070

Miami Passport Agency
Third Floor, Claude Pepper
    Federal Office Bldg.
51 S.W. First Ave.
Miami, FL 33130-1680
Recording: 305/536-4681

New Orleans Passport Agency
Postal Services Bldg., Room
    T-12005
701 Loyola Ave.
New Orleans, LA 70113-1931
Recording: 504/589-6728

New York Passport Agency
Room 270, Rockefeller Center
630 Fifth Ave.
New York, NY 10111-0031
Recording: 212/399-5290

Philadelphia Passport Agency
Room 4426, Federal Bldg.
600 Arch St.
Philadelphia, PA 19106-1684
Recording: 215/597-7480

San Francisco Passport Agency
Suite 200, Tishman Speyer Bldg.
525 Market St.
San Francisco, CA 94105-2773
Recording: 415/744-4444 or
    744-4010

Seattle Passport Agency
Room 992, Federal Office Bldg.
915 Second Ave.
Seattle, WA 98174-1091
Recording: 206/220-7788

Stamford Passport Agency
One Landmark Square
Broad and Atlantic Streets
Stamford, CT 06901-2767
Recording: 203/325-4402

Washington Passport Agency
1425 K St., NW
Washington, DC 20522-1705
Recording: 202/647-0518

APPENDIX C

Foreign Embassies in the United States

Contact the embassy of your host country for specific information about visa requirements for U.S. exchange students.

Embassy of Argentina
1600 New Hampshire Ave., NW
Washington, DC 20009
202/939-6400

Embassy of Australia
1601 Massachusetts Ave., NW
Washington, DC 20036
202/797-3000

Embassy of Austria
3524 International Court, NW
Washington, DC 20008
202/895-9700

Embassy of Bangladesh
2201 Wisconsin Ave., NW
Washington, DC 20007
202/342-8712

Embassy of Belgium
3330 Garfield St., NW
Washington, DC 20008
202/333-6900

Embassy of Belize
2535 Massachusetts Ave., NW
Washington, DC 20008
202/332-9636

Embassy of Bolivia
3014 Massachusetts Ave., NW
Washington, DC 20008
202/483-4410

Embassy of Brazil
3006 Massachusetts Ave., NW
Washington, DC 20008
202/745-2700

Embassy of Bulgaria
1621 22nd St., NW
Washington, DC 20008
202/387-7969

Embassy of Burundi
2233 Wisconsin Ave., NW
Washington, DC 20007
202/342-2574

Embassy of Cameroon
2349 Massachusetts Ave., NW
Washington, DC 20008
202/265-8790

Embassy of Canada
501 Pennsylvania Ave., NW
Washington, DC 20001
202/682-1740

Embassy of Chile
1732 Massachusetts Ave., NW
Washington, DC 20036
202/785-1746

Embassy of Colombia
2118 Leroy Place, NW
Washington, DC 20008
202/387-8338

Embassy of Costa Rica
1825 Connecticut Ave., NW
Washington, DC 20009
202/234-2945 .

**Embassy of the Czech
    Republic**
3900 Spring of Freedom St., NW
Washington, DC 20008
202/363-6315

Embassy of Denmark
3200 Whitehaven St., NW
Washington, DC 20008
202/234-4300

Embassy of Djibouti
1156 15th St., NW
Washington, DC 20005
202/331-0270

**Embassy of the Dominican
    Republic**
1715 22nd St., NW
Washington, DC 20008
202/332-6280

Embassy of Ecuador
2535 15th St., NW
Washington, DC 20009
202/234-7200

Embassy of Egypt
2310 Decatur Place, NW
Washington, DC 20008
202/232-5400

Embassy of El Salvador
2308 California St., NW
Washington, DC 20008
202/265-3480

Embassy of Estonia
9 Rockefeller Place, #1421
New York, NY 10011
212/247-1450

Embassy of Finland
3216 New Mexico Ave., NW
Washington, DC 20016
202/363-2430

Embassy of France
4101 Reservoir Road, NW
Washington, DC 20007
202/944-6000

Embassy of Germany
4645 Reservoir Road, NW
Washington, DC 20007
202/298-4000

Embassy of Ghana
3512 International Drive
Washington, DC 20008
202/686-4500

Embassy of Greece
2221 Massachusetts Ave., NW
Washington, DC 20008
202/332-2844

Embassy of Grenada
1701 New Hampshire Ave., NW
Washington, DC 20009
202/265-2561

Embassy of Guatemala
2220 R St., NW
Washington, DC 20008
202/745-4952

Embassy of Guinea
2112 Leroy Place, NW
Washington, DC 20008
202/483-9420

Embassy of Haiti
2311 Massachusetts Ave., NW
Washington, DC 20008
202/332-4090

Embassy of Honduras
3007 Tilden St., NW
Washington, DC 20008
202/966-7700

Embassy of Hungary
3910 Shoemaker St., NW
Washington, DC 20008
202/362-6730

Embassy of Iceland
2022 Connecticut Ave., NW
Washington, DC 20008
202/265-6653

Embassy of India
2107 Massachusetts Ave., NW
Washington, DC 20008
202/939-7000

Embassy of Indonesia
2020 Massachusetts Ave., NW
Washington, DC 20036
202/775-5200

Embassy of Ireland
2234 Massachusetts Ave., NW
Washington, DC 20008
202/462-3939

Embassy of Israel
3514 International Drive
Washington, DC 20008
202/364-5500

Embassy of Italy
1601 Fuller St., NW
Washington, DC 20009
202/328-5500

Embassy of Jamaica
1850 K St., NW
Washington, DC 20006
202/452-0660

Embassy of Japan
2520 Massachusetts Ave., NW
Washington, DC 20008
202/939-6700

Embassy of Jordan
3504 International Drive
Washington, DC 20008
202/966-2664

Embassy of Kazakhstan
3421 Massachusetts Ave., NW
Washington, DC 20008
202/333-4504

Embassy of Kenya
2249 R St., NW
Washington, DC 20008
202/387-6101

Embassy of Kyrgyzstan
1511 K St., NW
Washington, DC 20005
202/347-3732

Embassy of Latvia
4325 17th St., NW
Washington, DC 20011
202/726-8213

Embassy of Lithuania
2622 16th St., NW
Washington, DC 20009
202/234-5860

Embassy of Luxembourg
2200 Massachusetts Ave., NW
Washington, DC 20008
202/265-4171

Embassy of Malaysia
2401 Massachusetts Ave., NW
Washington, DC 20008
202/328-2700

Embassy of Mexico
1911 Pennsylvania Ave., NW
Washington, DC 20006
202/728-1600

Embassy of Morocco
1601 21st St., NW
Washington, DC 20009
202/462-7979

Embassy of Mozambique
1990 M St., NW
Washington, DC 20036
202/293-7146

Embassy of Nepal
2131 Leroy Place, NW
Washington, DC 20008
202/667-4550

Embassy of the Netherlands
4200 Linnean Ave., NW
Washington, DC 20008
202/244-5300

Embassy of New Zealand
37 Observatory Circle, NW
Washington, DC 20008
202/328-4800

Embassy of Nigeria
2201 M St., NW
Washington, DC 20037
202/822-1500

Embassy of Norway
2720 34th St., NW
Washington, DC 20008
202/333-6000

Embassy of Panama
2862 McGill Terrace, NW
Washington, DC 20008
202/483-1407

Embassy of Paraguay
2400 Massachusetts Ave., NW
Washington, DC 20008
202/483-6960

Embassy of the People's
Republic of China
2300 Connecticut Ave., NW
Washington, DC 20008
202/328-2500

Embassy of Peru
1700 Massachusetts Ave., NW
Washington, DC 20036
202/833-9860

Embassy of the Philippines
1617 Massachusetts Ave., NW
Washington, DC 20036
202/483-1414

Embassy of Poland
2640 16th St., NW
Washington, DC 20009
202/234-3800

Embassy of Portugal
2125 Kalorama Road, NW
Washington, DC 20008
202/328-8610

Embassy of Romania
1607 23rd St., NW
Washington, DC 20008
202/232-4747

Embassy of the Russian
Federation
1125 16th St., NW
Washington, DC 20036
202/628-7551

Embassy of Senegal
2112 Wyoming Ave., NW
Washington, DC 20008
202/234-0540

Embassy of Sierra Leona
1701 19th St., NW
Washington, DC 20009
202/939-9261

Embassy of Singapore
1824 R St., NW
Washington, DC 20009
202/667-7555

Embassy of Slovakia
2201 Wisconsin Ave., NW
Washington, D.C. 20007
202/965-5160

Embassy of South Africa
3051 Massachusetts Ave., NW
Washington, DC 20008
202/232-4400

Embassy of South Korea
2450 Massachusetts Ave., NW
Washington, DC 20008
202/939-5600

Embassy of Spain
2700 15th St., NW
Washington, DC 20009
202/265-0190

Embassy of Swaziland
3400 International Drive
Washington, DC 20008
202/362-6683

Embassy of Sweden
600 New Hampshire Ave., NW
Washington, DC 20037
202/944-5600

Embassy of Switzerland
2900 Cathedral Ave., NW
Washington, DC 20008
202/745-7900

Embassy of Thailand
2300 Kalorama Road, NW
Washington, DC 20008
202/483-7200

Embassy of Turkey
1714 Massachusetts Ave., NW
Washington, DC 20036
202/659-8200

Embassy of Ukraine
1828 L St., NW
Washington, DC 20036
202/333-0606

**Embassy of the United
    Kingdom of Great Britain
    and Northern Ireland**
3100 Massachusetts Ave., NW
Washington, DC 20008
202/462-1340

Embassy of Uruguay
1919 F St., NW
Washington, DC 20006
202/331-1313

**Apostolic Nunciature
    (Vatican City)**
3339 Massachusetts Ave., NW
Washington, DC 20008
202/333-7121

Embassy of Venezuela
1099 30th St., NW
Washington, DC 20007
202/342-2214

Embassy of Yugoslavia
2410 California St., NW
Washington, DC 20008
202/462-6566

Embassy of Zimbabwe
1608 New Hampshire Ave., NW
Washington, DC 20009
202/332-7100

Organizations Involved in Youth Exchange

These groups will serve as additional resources to learn about youth exchange programs, hosting opportunities, and international studies.

American Association of Collegiate Registrars and Admissions Officers (AACRAO)
One Dupont Circle, NW
Suite 330
Washington, DC 20036-1171
202/293-9161

AACRAO publishes the *World Education Series*—a comprehensive study of the educational systems of individual nations. Also, it produces materials to aid its members in assessing the credentials of international students entering U.S. schools.

American Association of School Administrators (AASA)
1801 N. Moore St.
Arlington, VA 22209
703/528-0700

AASA offers its members a "global perspectives kit," including audiovisual and printed materials like *Getting Started in Global Education: A Primer for Principals and Teachers* and *Global Education: A Personal Experience*.

Council of Better Business Bureaus
With more than 20 autonomous offices throughout the country, this nonprofit agency serves as a watchdog for local business, uncovering fraud and investigating consumer complaints. Your local BBB office could give you valuable information about individual exchange companies operating in your area.

Consumer Information Center
P.O. Box 100
Pueblo, CO 81002
The center distributes brochures like *Foreign Entry Requirements* to prepare exchange students for their trip abroad.

Council on International Educational Exchange (CIEE)
205 E. 42nd St.
New York, NY 10017
212/661-1414

CIEE offers several informative books for exchange students: *Going Places: The High School Student's Guide to Study, Travel Adventure Abroad, 1993–1994*; *Volunteer! The Comprehensive Guide to Voluntary Service in the U.S. and Abroad*; and *Work, Study, Travel Abroad 1992–1993: The Whole World Handbook*. Also, it issues (for a small fee) International Student Identity Cards which entitle students to discounts on transportation, insurance, and other expenses of an exchange trip.

Council on Standards for International Educational Travel (CSIET)
3 Loudoun St., SE
Leesburg, VA 22075
703/771-2040

CSIET is a non-profit group charged with establishing and maintaining standards for international educational travel programs, including youth exchange opportunities. Through its annual *Advisory List of*

International Educational Travel and Exchange Programs, it monitors compliance with these standards and shares information about exchange organizations operating programs for secondary students.

Institute of International Education (IIE)
809 United Nations Plaza
New York, NY 10017
212/883-8200

IIE serves as an information clearinghouse for all aspects of cultural and educational exchanges, primarily for postsecondary students.

International Exchange Association
1825 I St., NW
Suite 475
Washington, DC 20006
202/296-4777

The consortium will have answers to questions about exchange programs for adults—"citizen exchanges" such as groups of people moving between sister cities or professionals visiting their counterparts in other countries—as well as student exchanges.

Mobility International USA
P.O. Box 3551
Eugene, OR 97403
503/343-1284

This chapter of Mobility International strives to place more disabled people in ongoing exchange programs. It publishes *A World of Options for the 1990's: A Guide to International Educational Exchange, Community Service, and Travel for Persons with Disabilities*.

National Association for Foreign Student Affairs (NAFSA)
1875 Connecticut Ave., NW
Suite 1000
Washington, DC 20009
202/462-4811

NAFSA provides materials and training to help local schools deal with the care and placement of international exchange students in the United States. It publishes *Policy Statement on International Educational Exchange*, a guide to immigration laws and resource handbooks for teachers who work with international students.

National Association of Secondary School Principals (NASSP)
1904 Assocation Drive
Reston, VA 22091
703/860-0200

NASSP produces aids for educators dealing with youth exchange and international issues.

National Federation of State High School Associations (NFSHSA)
11724 NW Plaza Circle, Box 20626
Kansas City, MO 64195-0626
816/464-5400

NFSHSA will advise host families and schools about extracurricular activities for exchange students, notably the issue of eligibility in sports competition and other high school programs.

National School Boards Association (NSBA)
1680 Duke St.
Alexandria, VA 22314
703/838-6722

The NSBA videotape *NSBA Reports: The Global Connection* underscores the benefits of global education, depicting ways to develop a global perspective and to control bias.

U.S. Information Agency
Youth Program Division
301 Fourth St., SW
Room 357
Washington, DC 20547
202/619-6299

USIA's Youth Program Division works closely with exchange organizations, evaluating their applications for status as "Teenage Exchange Visitor Programs" and streamlining visa procedures for entering students. Also, they supervise the President's International Youth Exchange Initiative to publicize exchange programs in the United States.

APPENDIX E

Passport/Visa Services

Should you find yourself overwhelmed by applications for your passport and visa, these agencies specialize in processing the paperwork for you—for a fee. Contact individual companies for more information.

Embassy Visa Service
2162 California St., NW
Washington, DC 20008
202/387-1171

Mister Visa
211 E. 43rd St.
New York, NY 10017
212/682-3895

TransWorld Visa Service
790 27th Ave.
San Francisco, CA 94121
415/752-6957

Travel Agenda
119 W. 57th St.
Suite 1008
New York, NY 10019
212/265-7887

Visa Service, Inc.
581 Boylston St.
Boston, MA 02116
617/266-7646

APPENDIX F

Other Services

You can learn about the medical identification programs of the **Medic Alert Foundation** by calling 800/344-3226 or 800/432-5378.

For more tips on choosing suitcases, order a copy of *How to Select Luggage, Business Cases, and Personal Leather Goods* by sending $1 to the Luggage and Leather Goods Manufacturers of America, Inc., 350 Fifth Ave., New York, NY 10118.

APPENDIX G

Customs Procedures

You must declare everything that you have bought abroad and you have with you as you return to the United States. If the value of these items exceeds $400 (U.S.), then you will pay duty on them. Also, you can bring back only one liter of liquor or wine (if you are at least 21 years old when you return) and 200 cigarettes or 100 cigars. Outlawed materials include narcotics, obscene items, many animals, fruits and vegetables, meats, poultry, and other organic products. During your return flight, you should receive a simple customs form which asks for your name, address, and other personal information. If the total retail value of your purchases exceeds $1,400, you must list every item on the form. Otherwise, you do not have to list your purchases, but you should be ready to answer questions about them posed by customs officers.

You may mail back to your home packages containing your purchases, without paying duty on the gifts, if the value of each package does not exceed $50. You will be allowed one such package per day.

Bibliography

EXCHANGE PROGRAMS DESCRIPTIONS AND DIRECTORIES

Consumer Information Center. *One Friendship at a Time: Your Guide to International Youth Exchange*. Pueblo, Colo.: Consumer Information Center.

Council on International Educational Exchange. *Going Places: The High School Student's Guide to Study, Travel and Adventure Abroad*. New York: St. Martin's Press, 1993.

———*Work, Study, Travel Abroad: The Whole World Handbook*. New York: Council on International Educational Exchange, 1992.

Council on Standards for International Educational Exchange. *Advisory List of International Educational Travel and Exchange Programs, 1992–93*. Leesburg, Va.: Council on Standards for International Educational Exchange, 1992.

Grove, Cornelius L. *Orientation Handbook for Youth Exchange Programs*. Yarmouth, Me.: Intercultural Press, 1989.

Kinkhead, Katharine T. *Walk Together, Talk Together*. New York: Norton, 1962.

National Association for Foreign Student Affairs. *Building the Professional Dimension of Educational Exchange*. Yarmouth, Me.: Intercultural Press, 1988.

Steen, Sara J., and Ed Battle, eds. *Academic Year Abroad, 1991–92*. New York: Institute of International Education, 1991.

———*Vacation Study Abroad, 1991*. New York: Institute of International Education, 1991.

TRAVEL TIPS

Annand, Douglass R. *The Wheelchair Traveler*. Milford, N.H.: Annand Enterprises, 1979.

Kohls, L. Robert. *Survival Kit for Overseas Living*. Yarmouth, Me.: Intercultural Press, 1984.

Neumann, Hans H. *Foreign Travel Immunization Guide.* 12th ed. Montvale, N.J.: Medical Economics Co., 1987.

U.S. Department of Agriculture. Animal and Plant Health Inspection Service. *Travel Tips on Bringing Food, Plant and Animal Products Into the United States.* Washington, D.C.: U.S. Government Printing Office, 1987.

U.S. Department of State. *Foreign Entry Requirements.* Washington, D.C.: U.S. Government Printing Office, 1993.

———*Health Information for International Travel.* Washington, D.C.: U.S. Government Printing Office, 1992.

———*Tips for Travelers* (editions for the Caribbean, Central and South America, Cuba, Eastern Europe, Mexico, the Middle East and North Africa, People's Republic of China, South Asia, and Sub-Saharan Africa). Washington, D.C.: U.S. Government Printing Office, 1992.

———*Travel Warning on Drugs Abroad.* Washington, D.C.: U.S. Government Printing Office, 1987.

———*Your Trip Abroad.* Washington, D.C.: U.S. Government Printing Office, 1992.

U.S. Department of the Treasury. Customs Service. *Know Before You Go: Customs Hints for Returning U.S. Residents.* Washington, D.C.: U.S. Government Printing Office, 1991.

COUNTRY INFORMATION

Bair, Frank E., ed. *Countries of the World and Their Leaders Yearbook 1993.* Detroit, Mich.: Gale Research, Inc., 1993.

The Encyclopaedia Brittanica.

The World Book Encyclopedia.

World Chamber of Commerce Directory. Loveland, Colo.: World Chamber of Commerce Directory, Inc., 1993.

U.S. CULTURAL INFORMATION

Inge, M. Thomas, ed. *Handbook of American Popular Culture.* Westport, Conn.: Greenwood Press, 1993.

Lanier, Alison. *Living in the U.S.A.* Yarmouth, Me.: Intercultural Press, 1981.

INTERCULTURAL COMMUNICATIONS

Non-fiction

Axtell, Roger E., ed. *Do's & Taboos Around the World.* New York: Wiley, 1990.

Condon, John and Fathi Yousef. *An Introduction to Intercultural Communication.* New York: Macmillan, 1975.

Culture Shock (series of booklets dealing with individual countries). Portland, Ore.: Graphic Arts Center Publishing, 1992.

Gudykunst, William B. and Young Yun Kim. *Communicating With Strangers: An Introduction to Intercultural Communication.* New York: McGraw-Hill, 1984.

Hall, Edward T. *An Anthropology of Everyday Life.* Garden City, N.Y.: Doubleday, 1992.

———*Beyond Culture.* Garden City, N.Y.: Doubleday, 1977.

———*The Silent Language.* Garden City, N.Y.: Doubleday, 1973.

Samovar, Larry A., and Richard E. Porter. *Communicating Between Cultures.* Belmont, Calif.: Wadsworth Publishing Co., 1991.

Samovar, Larry A., and Richard E. Porter, eds. *Intercultural Communications: A Reader.* Belmont, Calif.: Wadsworth Publishing Co., 1991.

Fiction

Achebe, Chinua. *Things Fall Apart.* New York: Knopf, 1992.

Bowen, Elenore Smith. *Return to Laughter.* Garden City, N.Y.: Doubleday, 1964.

Durrell, Gerald. *My Family and Other Animals.* New York: Viking Penguin, 1977.

Lederer, William J., and Eugene Burdick. *The Ugly American.* New York: Norton, 1965.

LANGUAGE AIDS

Language tape series by AMR, Audioforum, Berlitz and Passport.

Rubin, Joan, and Irene Thompson. *How to Be a More Successful Language Learner.* Boston: Heinle and Heinle, 1982.

POST-EXCHANGE ACTIVITIES

Arpan, Jeffrey S. *Opportunities in International Business Careers.* Lincolnwood, Ill.: VGM Career Horizons, 1989.

Carland, Maria Pinto, and Daniel H. Spatz, Jr., eds. *Careers in International Affairs.* Washington, D.C.: School of Foreign Service, Georgetown University, 1991.

King, Nancy and Ken Huff. *Host Family Survival Kit: A Guide for American Host Families.* Yarmouth, Me.: Intercultural Press, 1985.

Rhinesmith, Hon. Stephen H. *Bring Home the World: A Management Guide for Community Leaders of International Programs.* New York: Walker & Co., 1986.

Index

H

Haiti 198
Hansen, John 80
Hansen, Randy 13
Hartwick College 9
health insurance 31–32
Herodotus 5
holidays and festivals 42
Holland 11
homestay concept 4, 22, 44
Honduras 198
Hong Kong 198
hospital birth record 28
host families 39, 43–47, 72, 87
Host Family Survival Kit 57–62
hosting an exchange student 78, 90–95
Huff, Ken 57–62, 72
Hungary 198
hygiene 51, 65

I

Iberoamerican Cultural Exchange Program 139–140
Iceland 198
Illinois 95
immersion (language training) 8
Immigration and Naturalization Service 27
immunoglobin 31
India 199
Indonesia 199
Institute of International Education 220
intensive study 22
Intercambio Internacional de Estudiantes, A.C. 141–142
international awareness 16–17
International Christian Youth Exchange 142–144
International Education Forum 144–146

International Exchange Association 220
International Student Exchange 146–148
International Travel Study 148–150
interpersonal communication 9, 75
INTRAX—International Training and Exchange 150–152
Ireland 199
Irish American Cultural Institute, The 152–153
Israel 199
Italy 5, 199–200

J

Jacobson, William "Bud" and Mary 94–95
Jamaica 200
Japan 9, 11, 47, 59, 88, 200
Jaycees 86
jet lag 58
Jordan 200

K

Kazakhstan *See* Commonwealth of Independent States
Kenya 201
King, Nancy 57–62, 72
Kiwanis 86
Korea (South) 201

L

language 8, 40, 47–48, 58, 83–84, 85, 92
"language fatigue" 58
Latvia *See* Baltic States
Legacy International 153–155
legal troubles 70–71
Leningrad 12